The Book of Thomas

A Guide for Life
and the Afterlife

*Channeled from a Spirit Guide
Named Thomas Bateman Who Refers to Himself as
"The Great Communicator"*

by
Daniel Aber & Gabreael

Cork Hill Press
Indianapolis

CORK HILL PRESS™

Cork Hill Press
7520 East 88th Place, Suite 101
Indianapolis, Indiana 46256-1253
1-866-688-BOOK
www.corkhillpress.com

Issued simultaneously in hardcover and trade paperback editions.
Hardcover Edition: 1-59408-506-4
Trade Paperback Edition: 1-59408-114-X

Library of Congress Card Catalog Number: 2003112927

Printed in the United States of America

1 3 5 7 9 10 8 6 4 2

Contents

Preface

In the early 1960s, I became fascinated with metaphysics, especially with hypnosis and meditation. I also experimented with energy transference and manipulation as well as a few other subjects. It was at that time, I also became aware that I was somewhat psychic. For several years, I worked with others using hypnosis to explore past life regression; behavioral modification and used my psychic ability to pass on information to friends. The information just seemed to pop out of nowhere.

Passing on psychic information to others was short lived. It became a catch twenty-two situation. Sometimes when I passed the information on to a friend, they would say, "Please don't tell me anything about the future or about anything that might happen later." Then when I withheld the information and the situation came to pass, I would get hell for not telling them. I learned in a short time to keep my mouth shut.

During the eighties and early nineties, I received "readings" from several other psychics; some over the phone, some by mail and others in person. Also, I was doing a lot of meditation and I was receiving a lot of information. I was told it was being given to me by my spirit guides. This information was somewhat profound and some of it challenged my religious and moral beliefs, as well as my limited understanding of life.

Having worked for several years as an Investigator for the U.S. Army Military Police, I was trained, to "Don't believe anything you hear and only about half of what you see." Using this ingrained method of thinking, I was suspect of the information I was receiving from my spirit guides and I just stored most of it away for later and in some cases, I just ignored it.

For the past few years I have been putting information together for a book about spirit. Again, not trusting the information I was receiving from the spirit realm, I decided to work with a psychic medium to channel the information I was seeking. After working with several so called psychics, I finally found one in Oklahoma, I will call Jeff. He seemed to have a positive connection with the other side and I worked with him for about a year, channeling nineteen one hour sessions. Most of that work was directed at talking with friends and relatives on the other side, that I already had a lot of information about and I knew I could verify a lot of the information I was getting. I also learned as an investigator, that the only way to really know if the information you are getting is true, was to ask some questions that you already had the answers to.

During some of our sessions, the information I was getting was somewhat suspect and since I had gathered most of the information I needed for the book, I decided to shop around for another psychic to verify some of the information I had received during those nineteen sessions with Jeff. Again, after some exploring, I was searching on eBay and came across a psychic named Gabreael. Her advertisement said "Get a Glimpse Through The Veil." I won one of her auctions and arranged for a reading over the phone. During this first session, I knew that something different was happening. Something different from any other psychic reading I ever experienced. Instead of getting answers to my prepared questions, I was getting information about myself that very few people knew about and certainly not Gabreael.

Our first session began on March 2nd, 2002 and our last scheduled session ended on November 4th, 2002. There were twenty-eight sessions that lasted about thirty minutes to an hour each in duration. It was during those sessions, the information for this book was channeled through Gabreael by a spirit guide that was assigned to me by the name of Thomas Bateman, who calls himself "The Great Communicator." After the last scheduled session on November 4th, 2002 we had five additional sessions in order to clear up several questions. These started on November 18th, 2002 and ended on February 22nd, 2003.

I had been instructed by Thomas in one of our sessions that once I started writing the book, additional information would be given to me and that has been so. You will find that some sessions are relatively short. This was done for a reason. Several times during the sessions, Thomas would tell us that the information being given is what is necessary at the time. Several questions that I asked during some of the sessions were not answered. Thomas would say; "What the masses need to know at this time is being given and the information is being given in the order the guides were directed to give it."

It was important that the information they gave for the book was not embellished in any way. They told me several times that when I actually started to put the book together, they would provide some additional information and answers to some previously asked questions. I have tried to provide all of the information just as it was presented to me and in the order it was presented.

The information provided, covers the actual birth of the soul. How and why man comes to Earth. What happens while you are here on Earth and why. What happens when you die and why it happens and one of the biggest questions of all; what happens after you die. The information explains Heaven and Hell and names the overseers that are in charge. For the first time ever, it will provide science with a starting point using DNA, to prove once and for all if we have lived more than one life on Earth. Such issues as murder, abortion, suicide, diseases, charting, dreams, prayer and the Christ Consciousness are explained. In addition issues such as angels, fallen angels, spirit guides and Universal Law are explained.

A Message From Spirit

The information in this book was channeled entirely from the spirit world. The authors of the book, Daniel and Gabreael, were instructed by the spirit guides not to try and defend the book because it was designed to defend itself.

While the book is not about religion, it was written in such a manor to challenge the belief system that you have accumulated during this lifetime as well as many other lifetimes. The book will raise many issues and questions with each individual that reads the material. You are encouraged by spirit, not to seek the answers you are looking for from "Man," but to seek answers directly from God through prayer and meditation. If you follow this course you will find your answers and this will be "your truth." It is written in the Holy Bible: Luke Chapter 11: Verses 9,10: "And I say unto you, ask and it shall be given you: seek, and ye shall find: knock, and it shall be opened unto you." "For every one that asketh, receiveth; and to he that seeketh, findeth; and to him that knocketh it shall be opened."

This book was designed to be a Guide for Life and the Afterlife. Once this book is published and distributed to the masses it will cause a shift in consciousness both in the physical dimension and the World of Spirit. Much of the information in this book has not been available to the souls in spirit. The information in the book has been given to "Man" and "Spirit" at this time, because this is what is needed now by the masses. Man/Soul must take responsibility for his/her actions or inactions. If you find yourself in a body or in a situation that you do not like, don't blame God. You, as an individual soul, choose this lifetime and the circumstances surrounding it. If you don't like who you are or where you are or what is happening to you, then change it; but you as an individual must finally accept responsibility for your life and everything in it. God did not put you here; you choose to come to Earth at this time, in this body, as well as the experiences you are being confronted with daily.

We highly suggest you read the book, then meditate and pray directly to God and you will receive a new truth that will guide you for the rest of your time in the physical dimension.

Go in peace. Seek in peace. Be in peace.

Introduction

Since the time Man first arrived on Earth, he has been asking; Who am I?; Why am I here?; Where did I come from?; What am I supposed to do?; What will happen when I die?; and a host of other questions. Over the years, much information has been disseminated to the masses on these subjects by psychics, educators and a host of others as well as information channeled from the spirit world. Some of the information is valid and has been useful to others. But a lot of misinformation has been presented and this misinformation has caused damage and confusion to a lot of unsuspecting souls.

A lot of the information presented in the past, especially channeled information, has been lengthy and difficult for the average person to understand. The information in this book was written as it was channeled and has been formatted in a form that is easy for the average reader to understand. That is not to say that everyone will agree with what is being given, especially if the information challenges your religious and moral beliefs as well as other understandings that you have collected for a lifetime.

It has been my belief, that in order to get answers, it helps to know in advance what questions to ask. This book will provide the reader with such questions. While the book will not answer all of your questions, it will provide the reader with the necessary tools to use in obtaining your own answers.

Several times during the taped sessions, Thomas would say, "I know a lot of people will disagree with what I am going to say or I know this will upset a lot of people, but this information is what is needed by the masses at this time. It is the truth and the truth will set you free."

The information in this book was channeled through a spirit guide by the name of Thomas Batemen, who refers to himself as "The Great Communicator," and two other spirit guides assigned to me by the name of Paula and Eon. Some information was provided by an angel named Habiel, who is also assigned to work with me. The information was channeled through a psychic medium named Gabreael over a period of time starting in March 2002 and ending in November 2002, consisting of twenty-eight recorded sessions with five additional sessions to clear up several questions.

During all the years I have worked with spirit guides, at no time has any of them ever given their full name or any information about them. I have been told by my guides that they are not permitted to give you that information and that Thomas has received special permission to give me that information about himself.

Not only did Thomas provide us with verifiable information about him and his last incarnation, but he supplied pictures as well. This is unheard of; a very rare occasion and to my knowledge this is the first time this has happened.

Thomas Bateman:
A Derbyshire Antiquary

Thomas Bateman was born in 1821 at Rowsley, in the Derbyshire Peak District. His archaeological career, though relatively brief, is noteworthy both for its abundance, and the fact that his barrow-openings in Derbyshire and Staffordshire provide virtually the only evidence for the early Medieval archaeology of the Peak District and the elusive Peak Dwellers.

Thomas's father, William Bateman, was an amateur antiquarian and pursued his pastime in accomplishing the excavation of a number of barrows on the family estate at Middleton. When William Bateman died in 1835 aged only 38, Thomas's upbringing and education were taken in hand by his grandfather. Thomas was educated at the non-conformist academy at Bootle, and from 1837 assisted in running the family estate, while in his spare time exploring the peakland, hunting, shooting, collecting flints and examining the many local ancient monuments. Bateman became a keen student of archaeology and read and was greatly influenced by Sir Richard Colt Hoare's seminal work *Ancient Wiltshire*.

In 1841, Thomas reached his majority and set up his own house in Bakewell. He pursued an illicit affair with Mary Ann Mason, the wife of a boatman on the Cromford Canal, and for a some years they lived together as husband and wife, though they never married.
Bateman's archaeological career began by observing the demolition of Bakewell's Medieval church. In 1843, he joined the newly formed British

Archaeological Association, set up as a reaction to the influence of the Society of Antiquaries. Bateman attended the Canterbury Archaeological Congress of 1844 with Mary Mason, passing her off as his wife.

At about this time, Bateman built his own country house, Lomberdale, at Middleton, where he continued to live with Mary Mason. The house incorporated many of the architectural fragments rescued from Bakewell Church and Bateman set up a museum there to hold his growing archaeological and ethnographic collection.

Barrow Digging 1845-1861

Bateman's career as a barrow digger began in the 1840's. While at the 1844 Canterbury Congress he, along with other delegates, excavated a number of barrows in the countryside around Canterbury. In 1845, Bateman excavated 38 barrows in Derbyshire and Staffordshire, and was dubbed the Barrow Knight in a poem by fellow antiquarian Stephen Isaacson. In 1845 and 1846 Bateman toured the north of England with Mary Mason, and carried out excavations in York, where construction of the new railway was levelling a part of the city walls.

Bateman's excavation techniques were crude, most of his barrow openings were accomplished in a single day. However, he displayed rudimentary understanding of stratigraphy, kept plans and detailed field-notes of his work, and drawings of the artefacts he excavated. His interpretation of his work was hampered by the fads of his day, much of his writing was concerned with the dubious pseudo-science of craniology, and he was not easily able to distinguish between prehistoric, Roman and Anglo-Saxon material from his excavations.

On the death of his grandfather in 1847, in order to meet the conditions of the will Bateman abandoned Mary Mason and married Sarah Parker, the daughter of the antiquarian William Parker.

In the late 1840's Bateman, now legitimately married and the inheritor of his grandfather's estate, settled into a life of dull Victorian respectability. His first book, *Vestiges of the Antiquities of Derbyshire* - a compilation of his own work and the publication of records of earlier barrow digging antiquaries - was published in 1847, though it proved no great success.

During 1848-9 Bateman excavated a further 50 barrows and began the dubious practice of employing proxies (such as Samuel Carrington) to open and report on barrows on his behalf.

In 1850, Thomas was taken ill and nearly died. After his recovery he became increasingly introverted and religious in outlook, taking on a gloomy piety which prompted his collaborator Charles Roach Smith to write to him commenting on his friend's despondency and morbid religious feelings.

Between 1851 and 1861 Bateman excavated a further 22 barrows. His four children were born during this period. On the birth of Bateman's first child, a son, in 1852, Roach Smith wrote prophetically "I hope your child will do you credit. Too often we find they turn out in spite of all care no great things."

Bateman's health declined throughout the 1850's and he died suddenly in 1861 just as his second book, *Ten Years' Diggings*, was published.

In subsequent years his son squandered his father's wealth in support of an easy lifestyle, selling off the contents of the museum at Lomberdale and most of the objects recovered from Bateman's barrow diggings. Fortunately, much of the material from Derbyshire and many of Bateman's papers and fieldnotes were bought by Sheffield Museum in 1893, for the substantial sum of £1600.

Bateman's son ended his life confined to an asylum as a dipsomaniac, truly no great thing.

Getting Started. The First Two Sessions
March 2, 2002 & April 16, 2002

When I first started working with Gabreael, it was my intention to verify some of the information that I had received from the psychic named Jeff. This information was going to be used for a book of poems I was writing about spirit. During the first session with Gabreael, I realized that I had finally made contact with a real psychic medium and instantly I had a feeling that something was about to happen that I had not planned for.

Our first session started on March 2nd, 2002 and our second session was on April 16th, 2002. It should be pointed out that Gabreael had a basic format for doing readings by phone. First of all, she requested that you not provide her with any information about yourself, except your first name. Before each session she would go into meditation to prepare for the session. At the beginning of each session, she would re-connect with spirit and who ever wanted to come through or wanted be recognized, was allowed to do so.

In the beginning of the first few sessions, the spirits that came through, identified themselves with a first initial and then they would give a first name.

During our first session, my father, grandfather and a male entity that I had worked with as a hospice patient presented themselves to us. A lady that I had worked with in spirit in the past by the name of Wanita and two spirit guides assigned to me by the name of Thomas and Paula also came through to us.

The guide named Thomas, began providing information about me. He explained that I had a major gift of being able to heal others and a minor gift of being intuitive. He went on to say that I had two strong past incarnations that were having an effect on this lifetime. One was a lifetime in Egypt and another lifetime in Atlantis. Thomas also mentioned that I had a lower back problem and another medical problem with the thyroid, which happens to be true.

During the session, I was provided with a bouquet of spring flowers by my former hospice patient as a sign of appreciation for helping him before his death and some additional personal information that only I was aware of.

Our second session started out somewhat like the first. Gabreael was sick today, having a problem with her throat and communications between her and the spirit world were some what difficult. Thomas and Paula, my spirit guides, made their presence known and my mother identified herself. She handed Gabreael a wilted pink rose, which was a way of making an apology. She was apologizing for some things that had happened during my childhood that she felt guilty about and not doing more to protect me from those experiences.

During this session, Thomas again talked about some of my medical problems and offered some advise on them. Paula offered a lot of personal information about me that Gabreael could not possibly have known about. I was told this was to give assurance and validation, that she Paula, actually knew me and was aware of my present surroundings and circumstances.

I was given the opportunity to ask questions after everyone had passed on their information and comments. During a personal meditation session, I was told that I had an angel named Habiel working with me and I wanted to verify that with Thomas.

Q. Dan. Is there an angel by the name of Habiel working with me at this time?

A. Thomas. Yes, he is around you and working with you. Thomas shows Gabreael a hand holding a quartz crystal. Habiel is symbolically giving me a quartz crystal to work with.

Q. Dan. Do I have other spirit guides working with me?
A. Thomas. Yes, several others.

Q. Dan. What are they helping me do?
A. Thomas. Recently they have been working with you on health and environmental issues.

It was obvious by now that the spirit guides were going to great length to insure me that they were real and they knew a great deal about me. I also had the feeling that they trusted Gabreael and they had a very positive connection with her. At this point, I decided to schedule a few more sessions and see where it led me.

May 20, 2002
Our 3rd Session

The Day of Apologizes. More Personal Information.

Gabreael was feeling much better today and communications between her and the spirit world were much better. I decided to mention for the first time that I was writing a book about spirit just to see if anyone would offer any comments. To my dismay, no one did.

While my original intention when I started working with Gabreael was just to verify some of the information I had received through Jeff. It was obvious we were headed in a completely different direction.

This session started with my father, mother and brother coming through. While I had communicated with all of them through Jeff, this time was different. The information was more detailed and personal in nature and only information that they could know.

A few days before this session, my brother had appeared before Gabreael and had caused some mischief by throwing some of her things around her house and just being a pest. Today he apologized to her and pointed out that he was just trying to get her attention. My father and mother were very chatty today. Both of them were apologizing for things that happened to me during childhood; things that both could and should have prevented but were to busy with their own lives to be bothered with mine.

My brother was also apologetic for some of his past transgressions while he was still here on Earth. While I did accept their apologies, I couldn't help but feel; why bother now, it's to late to change anything and it is just opening up hurts from the past. I guess it was just something they needed to get rid of to make them feel better and gave more validation for me.

Finally, Thomas came foreword and was showing Gabreael a newspaper. He explained that he had seen me in the newspaper recently talking about some environmental issues. He also mentioned the angel Habiel and pointed out that I had a giant crystal in my room next to me. This is a quartz crystal that weighs 30 pounds. He also talked about some of my health issues. I felt that Thomas was getting involved at the moment to lighten things up a bit, because the information shared by my brother and my parents was somewhat emotional for everyone at the time.

Immediately after that, my grandfather that I had been named after came through and apologized for not being there for me in the past. He knew that he could and should have done more to help me and my parents out of the mess they were in while they were all here on Earth. He also mentioned a poem that I had written about *"The Hour Glass."* He also passed on some more personal information and then withdrew.

I decided to ask a few questions.

Q. Dan. What rules do they live by in the spirit world?
A.Thomas. We will have a discussion about that in a later session.

Q. Dan. Are you allowed to use any and all information that you find out about someone in spirit? Can it be published even though it might be of a personal or sensitive nature?
A. Thomas. Yes, you can use whatever you get from them, otherwise the information would not have been given to you in the first place.

I had a lot more questions by now, but I felt that I was being urged to listen more and save the questions for later. This ended our third session, which again had been mostly a validation for me.

May 22, 2002
Our 4ᵗʰ Session

Paula and Messages From the Bridge.

Usually, before a session, Gabreael does a short meditation to tune into spirit. Once in a great while she goes into a deep trance before a session. She explained to me that she rarely does this because she has some difficulty doing deep trance meditations and they leave her drained.

We also had a conversation before this session about a special bridge that I had an experience on in the late 1960s and several more experiences within the last two years. The experiences were too profound to try and explain here. This bridge will be explained in much greater detail in a future book, but it is necessary to mention it at this time because of what happened during this session. In our conversations, we refer to it as "The Bridge."

Before this session, Gabreael did go into a deep trance meditation and this is what happened. Gabreael explained to me that the last time she talked with me, she felt the presence of a very strong female but she wouldn't come forward or offer her name. This morning she did come forward. She is a spirit guide of Dans'. Her name is Paula. She is the type of guide that makes me Gabreael, feel uncomfortable. She is what I call a flyer. I tried to write down as much information as I could of what I saw for you.

Gabreael continued to say; that when we started out, it was like we were going down someone's eye. Paula started showing me religious stuff. It was Pagan, like earthy stuff. She did go into a past life connection of yours. She also showed me a mirror which meant reflection. We were flying and we landed on the Bridge, the one you sent me the pictures of.

She showed me a being, like the outskirts of a young man. It had two sides like being split in two. One side was very shinny and the other side was dark. We looked down into the water and it was very dark. All of a sudden a body came out of the water holding a candle. The body was surrounded in light. As I looked around, the body of the young man split in two and was gone.

Even though the body that came out of the water was surrounded in light, it had a dark shadow following it that looked like a mist. I asked Paula what this dealt with and why was the mist following this person. At the time, I was sure it was you Dan. She explained to me that this was a kind of cosmic residue, containing past, unresolved issues. She also showed me a grave which meant past issues that were buried very deep in the soul.

Paula went on to tell me that you had incarnated off the fifth level and that you were a teacher or some kind of manager in the spirit realm before coming into this lifetime. She said it would be hard to understand, that while your life went down the path it did at first, that it was what you choose to experience. She said that you needed to complete those experiences to add to your soul bank. Paula said that while your journey has been long, you have done very well. She said while you have been a male in most of your incarnations, you have lived lives in the physical dimension as both male and female. She also said that the mate you are presently with is your first lifetime together.

Paula went on to add, that you have experienced many lifetimes in the physical dimension (Earth). She said that you lived a lifetime in Egypt and one as a Celt and these life experiences are having a strong influence on this incarnation. She also stated that, "If you don't deal with the past, how can you face the future little one." She also explained to me that some of your health issues were predestined and some are not.

She went on to show me a zodiac wheel, which means destiny. I got the intense feeling that Paula is not around you a whole lot of the time. She is really strong and the kind that I, Gabreael, am afraid of because of her strength and power. When I first came out of meditation, I had a headache. I got the number two concerning Paula. Thomas is on my right at this time and he is giving me the number two, saying that Paula is from the upper echelon and the kind of guide that other guides get instructions from.

Thomas went on to say, that when Paula showed me the mirror, that was a reflection from your past and an inner reflection on you, Dan. He also said that the younger man that was lit up and split in two, indicated your two sides. He explained to me that when you were younger, you had a dark side and a light side. He said that you have overcome a lot and have learned a tremendous amount in this lifetime. Thomas is saying that I, Gabreael, would never have gotten along with you Dan, when you were younger and that I would have been afraid of you. He is saying that, yes you did come from the fifth level into this incarnation and that when you return to spirit you will go to either the fifth or sixth level.

At this point in our session, Thomas wants to know, if I Dan have any questions.

Q. Dan. Does Thomas feel that the past issues in my life that have not been dealt with, need to be dealt with at this time?
A. Thomas is making me feel like I have a heartache, like someone that has been hurt severely and emotionally. He is saying to me: "How can you possibly get over some things here in the physical body. When you are in spirit you see the completion of things, but in the physical dimension in the physical body, you don't. He is also telling me that he has played a role with some of your health issues; because while you, Dan, have tried to deal with a tremendous heartache and hurt and even though you have dealt with that, sometimes you just can't deal with those kinds of issues in the physical body. Thomas is saying to me, Gabreael, that you, Dan, have two loves in your life. Your wife and your biological son.

Thomas is also addressing the zodiac wheel. He says this addresses the many incarnations you Dan, have had. It is an indication of destiny and of future things to come. He says that the zodiac is put on a wheel in a circle because it is never ending and that all life is the same way. Past, present and future destiny. There is no cheating the test.

This was a very long session and by now it was obvious to me that Thomas and Paula wanted me to know that they were both very much in tune to my past, present and future and that they were going to remain connected to me for a while to come. While I wanted to ask about what was meant by the different levels they had mentioned, I had a feeling that I should wait and that I would understand that when the time was right for me to know.

May 23, 2002
Our 5th Session

Wish Out and Life in Spirit.

The session today started with Gabreael talking about the weather and her fish pond. She is fretting over having to clean out the pond and planting some new vegetation for the fish.

Thomas has stepped foreward and is saying something about Brian. Thomas just wants you, Dan, to know that you will be meeting someone by the name of Brian shortly, who will help you a great deal. This will be an important relationship in you life.

Thomas is heading downstream which means he is dealing with things of the past. He says that you are progressing well with your inner work. You are now at a time of reflection in your life. You find yourself homesick at times and desire to return to spirit. He says that he is worried that you will be a wish out. You are on the border of doing what is necessary to leave your present life and return to spirit. Thomas explains that a wish out is someone that, for whatever reason, is unhappy with his or her present life and has come to a realization that he or she could take the necessary steps to end the present life and in doing so, would be returned to the spirit world.

Thomas is heading further downstream. He is saying that your fascination with crystals is due to a lifetime in Atlantis and Bimini. Your lifetime there went fast. You worked with communications. Crystal energy was used for communications as well as many other applications. That civilization became very advanced in technology and the use of crystals. They started to use crystal power for negative uses and to control other people. That is what eventually led to the destruction of Atlantis.

Q. Dan. Could you explain a little more about being a wish out and what I need to do to change that?
A. Thomas. You need to be more zealous, more interested in life and in living. You need to address those issues and especially the depression.

Thomas wants to tell you something else because he feels you have been wondering much about this information. When you are in spirit, if you meet someone you did not like or get along with in your lifetime on Earth or if they did something to you, all the events surrounding that situation are presented so you can fully understand more about what happened or why. We mainly stay the same sex, but we do incarnate in other sexes just for the experience. It is a choice we have when we are in spirit.

Q. Dan. What is the family structure like in spirit?
A. Thomas. You are united with everyone over time.

Q. Dan. What kind of things are friends and relatives in spirit allowed to do or tell you about?
A. Thomas. There are individuals in spirit trained just to work with incarnates. If everyone knew about past incarnations or what they did in past lives it would be mass confusion. Only communicators that are trained for that are allowed to give you advice, etc. If people knew everything they did in past lives they would not be responsible for their actions because they would feel they could get away with everything and pay for it later. There are only selected communicators that work in selected areas to help others because your time is short on Earth, in the physical dimension. Earth is a learning ground and you need to focus on the events that you choose before being reincarnated. Eventually you become "full knowledge" in spirit.

Q. Dan. In the past I have experimented with astral projection. Is it possible to go directly to the spirit world and visit with friends and relatives there?
A. Thomas. Yes, it is possible, but it must be approved first.

Q. Dan. How do you get approved and by whom?

A. Thomas. By a counsel of elders. When there is an important journey to accomplish, such as life and death situations. Those kind of things. If everyone was allowed to do it, that would cause mass confusion.

Q. Dan. Do individuals sleep in spirit?

A. Thomas. No, but they do rest.

Q. Dan. Are people in spirit aware of God?

A. Thomas. Yes. The light that shines in spirit is not the Sun, but the light shinning off of God.

Thomas says that when souls in spirit have sex it is called merging. There are two different types of merging. A more intimate merging which is like what we call sex in the physical dimension on Earth. Then there is a more casual merging where you can see inside of them and they can see inside of you.

An individual soul can incarnate fifty times or more and have fifty or more different mates. We all have souls that we share common interests with and we also have split aparts. There has been a lot of misinformation disseminated about this. You don't spend a whole lifetime with just one person because you would miss out on many interactions and would not learn very much. Like ice cream with different flavors. If you only tried vanilla you would have no idea what the other flavors taste like. Some of these meetings or interactions are outlined in your chart before incarnating. At times, the soul will choose to pick a mate early on in an incarnation and stay true to that mate for that whole lifetime. At other times, the soul will choose during charting, to experience several encounters with other souls, just to add experience to the soul bank.

During different incarnations, we do meet up with other souls from other lifetimes and interact with them on different levels. Eventually, when all the incarnations are over, you do meet up with your soul mate. We also do not incarnate as animals or insects.

In this session, it became obvious to me that Thomas wanted me to know that they are around us a lot and they know what we are thinking and the questions we have. Some of the questions he addressed in this session I had written down on a piece of paper before the session. Most of the questions he addressed, I had been thinking about for some time, but I wasn't sure I should ask them.

Order in the Spirit World.

   Thomas is here today. He is saying that communications are difficult. They are showing me a snake. Does this mean anything to you?

   Thomas wants to clarify some issues. He knows that you Dan, have been trying to understand and to communicate with them. You have waned off your life path a little, but this was mostly due to you loosing your zeal or love of life on the Earth. Once you are back into atonement, communications will get better for you. They will not be perfect, but much better than they are at this time. On the beginnings of the new moon communications will also improve.

   Gabreael is saying that she hears horses and she just got a flash of a man next to a carriage with long dark hair. It might have been a flash of Thomas in his last incarnation. Something about 200. Thomas is saying he wants to address and clarify some questions that you Dan, have, but did not ask yet. He is saying something about traveling. He says that he teleports himself through space and time with number coordinates. He wants to clarify the order in the spirit world.

God the Father Head and Jesus
Counsel of Elders
Archangels
Spirit Guides
Mayors

Teachers etc.

There are seven levels of order in the spirit realm which people on Earth refer to as Heaven.

The first and second levels are for orientation of new souls just arriving from a past life on Earth.

The third level is an adjustment level. Souls need a period of time to adjust from being in the physical body. It takes a person a period of time to make the adjustment back to spirit.

The forth level is reserved for great minds, writers, artists etc.

The fifth level assists the first and second levels. They are teachers of science and such.

The sixth level helps the first, second, fourth and fifth levels. They are mostly organizers, teachers, managers and leaders. Dan came from the fifth level into this incarnation.

The seventh level is for the God head. Thomas says that he doesn't know very much about this level, other than he knows that this is the level that every soul strives to reach.

Thomas says to think of their hierarchy and government as a Greek democracy. He says that archangels do take on human form from time to time, however they were never human. They also take on a bright light form; almost glowing at times. The archangels are somewhat of a mystery and keep mostly to themselves. They are protectors of richness and usually stay on the seventh level.

There is a lot of misinformation that has been disseminated about the elders. They often appear to us in dreams and visions. Then often appear as older men but only for our benefit. In the spirit dimension, they enact policies and such. There is some work being put out saying that the elders were never human or lived on the Earth. This is just not true. How could they guide if they were never on the Earth plane. They could not. Even the archangels are on the Earth frequently. There is a lot of misinformation regarding this matter.

Q. Dan. Briefly, during one of our sessions you mentioned that I came here to be a healer. Could you tell me more about that and the mechanics of healing other people?

A. Thomas. You must learn to heal yourself before you can start healing others. When you work on healing others you also heal yourself. First you must remove the doubt that you have about your ability to heal others. You Dan, have the mind of a Alchemist. You need to buckle down to homeopathic healing. A combination of this and the crystals you work with will give you the mind, body and soul connection you will need to become a successful healer. Thomas wants you to understand something else as well. He says that you Dan, have overcome a lot as far as illness goes and you have learned from these experiences.

It was obvious from the information given by Thomas that he has been reading my mind again and decided to answer a lot of my questions without me having to ask. In one way, this is great, but looking at it from another direction it is a little unsettling to know that a spirit can read your mind whenever they desire to do so. Along with validation, I feel that Thomas wanted to convey that message to me.

May 30, 2002
Our 7ᵗʰ Session

A Great Gift Today. Thomas Reveals Who He Really Is.

This is the first time that Thomas reveals himself and tells us who he really is.

Gabreael is experiencing a bad thunder and lightning storm this morning and communications with the spirit world are somewhat difficult.

I am feeling several around you today. Of course, Thomas is present but I am getting a very strong vibration from a C. He is going to come through first. Calvin, his name is Calvin. Do you know anyone in spirit by that name? He is saying to tell Ralph and Dan hello. He is saying that your father is also here today and you Dan are going to receive a great gift today or something about a great gift today. He has a cane or some kind of staff and seems to be pounding it on the ground as if to get our attention. Do you know what this means? It feels like they are trying to tell you to pay special attention to what is being said today.

Q. Dan. Would you ask Calvin about the Bridge? Is that some kind of portal or something like that?
A. Calvin. The Bridge is a portal for communications for you because of your past experiences on the Bridge with him (Calvin).

Your father is not stepping forward, but I can feel his presence. Thomas is stepping up. Thomas says hello. I am seeing a great gift and something about doubt. Do you know what he is talking about? He is showing me a watch and is saying it is time. He is saying it is time to know who he is. He is saying that he was a Great Antiquarian. I am seeing an old church. Thomas Bateman, Thomas Bateman, he is saying Thomas Bateman over and over.

He is saying that he was English and that you and he have a kinship in that he loves buildings and art and that you have a love for the land, history and art. Thomas is saying that he has been given permission to give this information about him to you Dan at this time. This is a great gift, telling you who he is. This is something that spirit guides are never allowed to do.

He is saying something about writing; he was a writer as will you Dan be a writer. Thomas Bateman 61; 1861 is a prominent date for him. Be peaceful about it he says. He can communicate well with Gabreael as he knows her and she will know him when she sees him. He is saying that this is not a common thing for a spirit guide to give you his or her real name, or provide information about himself.

This is a great gift to you Dan. You have been given this information so you can set your doubts aside, since you Dan, have a problem believing the information you receive from spirit. This will help to validate the information and remove your doubts. Go in peace. Seek in peace.

Thomas is saying that he had one wife and one love. Seek and you will find all of this information about him. He is saying something about writing. I am getting these flashes and they are fast. I am getting something like a large church. Really old looking architecture. He is saying something about Middleton or Middletown. Thomas is showing me a library and saying, a great gift. I think he is saying he will be easy to find. It will be easy for us to find out information about him. He is also saying something about writing a book or something like that.

Thomas is saying something about William. Thomas wasted a lot of time in his past life. His life went fast. He just wasn't very happy at times. He is saying something about assisting you Dan with writing.

I am getting digging like with a shovel but I am not sure what he is trying to say. This is some kind of great affirmation that he is giving you Dan today. Like do it now. Do it now. He wants you to seek him out or look him up today. He is saying that is important, that this a very rare connection. You will know me when you see me. He is assisting you Dan, with writing.

Thomas was a writer but this was not his main occupation. He is showing me flashes of a big church. He is to assist you with soul searching and writing. He says that in most of your incarnations, you Dan, were a man and in most of his incarnations he was a man. He is saying over and over; a great gift: excitement: value: worth. We don't fully understand the value or worth of what he is giving us today.

I am getting horses again. I am getting the feeling I am riding and someone is behind me and I can't see who it is. He is saying one thing at a time. This is going to be a mind blowing experience. Something personal for you Dan. You are going to write a book and call it "The Book of Thomas."

I am getting a seal or crest of some kind. Something like a family crest. I don't know what this means. Thomas is saying something about him being a blue blood or something like that and something about diggings. He is saying go in peace, seek in peace and speak of him in peace.

I am getting like a birthday or some kind of bond or relationship. I am also getting the name Sarah. Thomas is showing me something about Sarah. He was not fond of her. He was married to Sarah but he was in love with Mary. He is showing me a jigsaw puzzle and putting the pieces together.

Well, Thomas was right. This was a mind blowing experience for both me and Gabreael. I have been working in the metaphysical field since 1963. I have worked with many physics over the years and I have worked with many spirit guides, both mine and others; I have channeled guides and other entities and I have chatted with many friends and relatives in the spirit dimension. Never have I experienced any guide or spirit giving any information about himself and never a full name or information that could be verified. This was a first and it was something that myself or Gabreael had never experienced before.

Of course, we did go to the computer and the world wide web. All I did was type in the name; Thomas Bateman and the information about him in the front of the book is what came up. There was a lot more information about him that you can look up yourself at the same web site if you desire to know more about Thomas. As Thomas said, this was truly a great gift and now I know why we are getting this information and what we are supposed to do with it. Write a book.

Back in the early eighties, I was doing a lot of work with my spirit guides through meditation and it was during that time that they were giving me a lot of information. The information was similar to what Thomas has given me so far. Because I was getting the information first hand from the guides and because a lot of the information was very controversial, I felt I was just making it all up in my own mind and I cut off the connection to that source and just ignored what I had already been given. It is obvious to me now that this is what Thomas was referring to in this session. I need a lot of validation before I will accept anything I receive from the spirit dimension and sometimes I need to hear it through a third person.

By the time you read the rest of this book you will understand why I was reluctant the first time to believe it. Even now, with all the work I have accomplished with the spirit world, I don't just believe everything I hear without some proof or verification and that includes some of the information in this book. By the time you read the rest of this book, I guarantee it will test your belief system. I have been told by Thomas, that is just what the book is intended to do. He has said that a vast majority of people need to hear this information at this time and for those people, it will be their truth.

June 4, 2002
Our 8th Session

Thomas, Paula and Habiel
Gold Star, Quill Pen, Gold Key and the Bridge.

As usual, Gabreael has just come out of meditation as she does for every session.

I went into deep meditation this morning and came in contact with Paula, another one of your spirit guides. We were on a bridge, the one you sent me the pictures of. I was going to fall and Paula took my hand and patted it like to say, no. After that, she took my hand and we dove straight down, head first into the water and we went upstream against the current. I could feel the strength of the current and the bubbles rushing against me. We were going really fast and I could hardly breathe. All of a sudden we hit shallow water and she pulled me up. She was completely dry and I was totally drenched. She handed me a very beautiful gold star.

You know how most stars have five points or whatever. This one was not like that. It had many, many points. I don't know how to describe it. It was very pointy and round. It was beautiful and lit up everything around us. When I looked back down at it, the star turned into a golden key. Then Paula spoke for the first time and said, this is what you and Dan are going to do with Thomas. She said, where much is given, much is required. Then she kissed me on both of my cheeks and vanished. At that point, I woke up.

Paula is a lot different from Thomas. Thomas is here now with an angel named Habiel. Thomas is going to explain to me what I saw. He says that going up stream is to go against the current, the normal in life. The pressure I felt was to push ahead, to push on. The star was a great gift. The key was to unlock the mystery of truth. He said the kiss was because I was doubly blessed.

Thomas is saying that great times are now upon us and there will not be much playtime any longer for you Gabreael and Dan. He says that Habiel has something to show us.

I am getting a door and a lot of light. I can't see Habiel, just a lot of light and in the mist of it, is a really big sword. It is turning into a pen with a big feather on the tip of it, like a big quill pen. The door is closing and I don't feel him any longer.

I am getting like a buzzing sound. I can still feel Thomas, but it is like he is doing something. He says that the pen is more mighty than the sword. The pen will overcome conflict. Be peaceful. Speak in peace. Do not be afraid, that the pen is truly more mightier than the sword.

The time has come to work. There is going to be a heavy, heavy load. Much work to be done. Not much play time for you and Dan and not much for Thomas either. Much to be revealed. Much to think about. Much to study about. A great gift. A great gift has been given. Much work to come. Ponder and think upon this. Much change. Change can be scary but you need to rest now and ponder and think on what's about to start. What's about to begin. Go in peace. Seek peacefully. Ponder and be peaceful. Much more to come.

I knew that at this point we had crossed over the line and nothing would be the same again. I knew now that there was no turning back. I wasn't quite sure yet what was about to come, but I knew it was of great importance with a lot of work attached to it and it was all a little scary. Over the past years, I have been cautioned by a lot of people who have advised me, "Be careful of what you ask for because you might just get it." Up until this time that hadn't made a lot of sense to me, but some how it just hit home. I couldn't help but wonder if I was going to be up to what was about to come and how I might react under the pressure. It became obvious to me that we were dealing with a once in a lifetime event, in uncharted waters, being led by someone in the spirit world, a spirit who we couldn't really see and could only feel his energy. I also knew that this would be a great test of faith. A test that had been put to me previously by the spirit world and one that I ran away from. I could only hope that wouldn't happen this time.

June 6, 2002
Our 9ᵗʰ Session

Thomas and Communications

This session starts as usual with Gabreael coming out of meditation. Communications are a little difficult today because of the weather.

Thomas and somebody else I haven't felt before is here today. I am getting an R and she is standing out before me, which means she stands out before you, but not a relative. This is a young female. She has overcome a great sadness. She is around you and she has heard you. She is giving me another initial; S, like she has two names or something. (Rosie) She is called Rosie but her real name is Sarah. Again she says she has heard you. She is presenting herself as an older woman now. She feels very peaceful now. She hands you a red rose, which means she loves you. She loves you like a brother. She is fading out.

Thomas is coming forword. He says hello. He is saying that you are doing better and something about a book. Something like a new book you are getting or something. He is showing me a moon and the signs Gemini and Aquarius. He is saying something about the moon from Gemini to Aquarius. He is trying to say something about much to be accomplished or given and communications will be better when Gemini and Aquarius are in alignment. You Dan, need to start preparing for much to be given. It will be something astounding starting with Aquarius to Gemini, the calendar dates of June 10ᵗʰ, to June 30ᵗʰ.

Thomas is saying something about you getting a book with the moon cycles so you can schedule sessions with the moon cycles for better communications and you need to start preparing for much work. There is going to be a big surprise, something amazing is going to take place about a belief system and a challenge. He Thomas will become a little more in tune with Dan. Thomas wants to know if you have more questions.

Q. Dan. How long has Thomas been working with me as a spirit guide?
A. Thomas. About three years.

Q. Dan. What do I need to write about?
A. Thomas. Where much is given, much is required. In time all things are known. You already know about denial and what you have done in the past is just a preparation for what is to come.

Q. Dan. Why is it necessary for me Dan to go through a psychic/medium in order to talk with him?
A. Thomas. When your body comes into atonement you will be able to communicate better with the spirit world. You Dan, need your mind to be in a much better state. In time all things will come to pass.

Q. Dan. Did Thomas and I ever share a lifetime together?
A. Thomas. No, but you will know him from a past lifetime.

Q. Dan. Are there any issues that stem from a past lifetime that I need to work on now or clear up?
A. Thomas. You have been penned up where you are now and you are dealing much better with that at this time. You really had a bad time about six years ago and for the three years he has been working with you, you have been able to clear out a lot.

Like many communications with the spirit world, sometimes all you get is a question for your question or you get a lot of riddles and very few answers. This has been one of the reasons that I haven't trusted the information from the spirit World more in the past. I am sure that they have their reasons for doing this but it can be frustrating at times.

It seems like Thomas is trying to prepare Gabreael and myself for what is about to come and he seems a little nervous in doing so. I am sure that you can appreciate the fact that she and I are getting a little nervous ourselves. Thomas keeps telling us we need to get prepared, but prepared for what.

The person that appeared in the beginning of the session (Rosie) is a person I was raised with after my parents separated when I was about eight years old. She considered me a brother and after she passed over to spirit I made contact with her and helped her to go fully into spirit and deal with some lingering problems she had become afraid to face. I am sure that this was just another validation from Thomas to get me to accept and trust the information he was presenting.

June 11, 2002
Our 10th Session

Beginning of the Soul

Our session starts today with a beautiful Carolina morning. Cool, but nice.

Thomas is present. He says greetings and that communications are much better now. June 10th to June 30th ends in Aquarius. Communications are better now because it is a new moon, ending in a full moon which always means better communications.

He says we will start at the beginning with the soul. God the Father is both male and female, as one. The soul is created in his image. Dually as both male and female. There is another half of us. This is where the term soul mate comes from. Everything was as before. Take a tree in spring time, growing and producing lots of leaves and now it is fall and the leaves are dying. Leaves stay but a season and the tree is barren. Then in the spring it starts to produce little buds again. This happens in cycles just as human life does. Rarely do two soul mates incarnate together because it usually causes confusion and is not productive. Often one half of the soul remains in spirit while the other half is in an incarnation and then both halves join again in spirit between incarnations.

Kindred souls: We are given kindred souls in a lifetime to learn and bond with. Kindred souls incarnate often in cycles. That is why one person is attracted to another even when they have not met before in this lifetime. When both sides of the soul (soul mates) incarnate together at the same time, not much is accomplished. They feed off each other and one side usually wants to become dominant over the other. Life on Earth or the physical dimension, is about growth.

There has been a lot of misinformation put out on the soul and soul mates and there has been to much emphasis put on soul mates. Life is about experience and growth. This must be understood. Thomas says there are five basic parts to the soul.

1. Soul birth. We are sparks of God, sparks of the Divine.

2. Soul Development. Mapping out or writing a chart of our lives for each incarnation. This requires much work and seems never ending. The soul is in constant development to the fifth stage. Remember: Development = growth.

3. Incarnation. The human experience and knowledge. With growth comes knowledge. You must have experiences to have growth and knowledge.

4. Going Home. This is when you return to spirit and go to the different levels; what humans call Heaven. You return to one of six of the seven levels.

5. Completion or completeness. This is what all souls aspire to. To reach the seventh level of the seven levels. Thomas doesn't know very much about the seventh level. This is the level where the soul returns to God.

Q. Dan. A soul mate is a manifestation of the self, not too separate souls. Is that correct?

A. Thomas. Yes. The soul splits in half at birth. The soul is born both male and female. They are two separate entities which make up the whole of the soul. We usually incarnate as either male or female, but we do experience both. Sometimes you will experience a deep longing. You may have a spouse and be in deep love, but suddenly a deep longing or emptiness occurs. This is the time when your soul mate is near, but it is not good for the soul mate to come around, because it usually ends up causing confusion.

A lot of misinformation has been written and exchanged about soul mates. Many people believe it is the ultimate experience to finally meet your soul mate in a particular incarnation and that life will be perfect from then on. Wrong; nothing could be further from the truth. In most cases, that is the last thing you would want to happen. As we have just told you, and we feel we should say it again. When the soul is born, it splits in half and there is a male and a female side. It is possible and happens often, that both sides incarnate at the same time into separate bodies; however each half takes on it's own personality as soon as it enters the physical body. Each half has a chart of it's own to follow, with different interests and goals.

If the two halves met during the same incarnation, there would be a contest to decide which half would be dominant. In most cases this would result in a serious conflict because each half has it's own agenda or life path to follow and it would be a conflict of interest to merge with the other at that time. In very few cases would one half want to give up it's dominance and give in totally to the other. I am sure you can see by now, the conflict in meeting your soul mate while you are incarnate. When you return to spirit, the whole process is different and the two halves do connect or integrate into one.

It is also possible that the soul could and sometimes does, split into more than two halves and live several physical lives (incarnations) at the same time. While this is very unusual, and does not happen very often, it does happen and it is not recommended.

You must remember that the primary purpose for each incarnation is to add experiences and information to the soul bank. When the soul returns to spirit, it becomes aware of every lifetime and also aware of all the experiences in the soul bank.

There is much misinformation and misunderstanding about this. Remember that in the beginning, the soul is created in God's image, which is love and light. This means that the soul is created in God's image, not the physical body. The physical body does not look like God.

Before each incarnation on the Earth plane, the soul enters a physical body in order to experience the things that are possible only on the Earth plane. Once that incarnation is over, the soul leaves the physical body and returns to spirit, where it started from. While the physical body is not immortal, the soul is. The soul will not and cannot, ever die. It is a part of God.

Remember, little one, much has been given to reflect upon. Go in peace. Seek in peace.

June 13, 2002
Our 11th Session

The Soul and Kindred Spirits

Dan had a hypnosis session today before this session and met Jesus at the Sea of Galilee.

Thomas is saying that he is changing the discussions for today. He will discuss the recognition of the soul.

The vessel, the body you are contained in is a combination of other lives. A child is born into a family, looking different than anyone in the family. No matter what vessel you are in, remember always, that the physical body is nothing more than a means of transportation in the physical dimension, the Earth. It is just a vessel, nothing more.

A Soul: You may have recognized a soul or person in the physical body, never having known that person before. The old saying is, "The eyes are the window to the soul." This is a true statement. When the soul is inside the human vessel and you come upon a kindred soul, a physical reaction takes place in the inner eye, brain and heart. The more developed psychically you are the stronger this is. It causes symptoms, and something happens to the eye, heart and brain. Sometimes a light headedness or queasiness results even though you have never known or met this person before.

This is what you have questions about. A kindred spirit is a spirit in your circle of spirits. Someone you would readily relate to. Looking in the eyes, gives you an instant knowing. Soul recognition is important.

Because of all the questions Dan has, Thomas will change his plans for today. Dan has many questions today after his experience with hypnosis just before the session and this has caused Thomas to put aside some of the information he had planned on giving us today.

Q. Dan. Why does God want us to worship him?
A. Thomas. On the Earth plane it's called worship, not elsewhere. It is living, progressing, or going toward completeness. Only on the Earth level or in the physical dimension where you are at now do we call it worship.

Q. Dan. Do Heaven and Hell really exist?
A. Thomas. Seven levels of the planes are what we call Heaven. Hell is real and he, Thomas will explain in more detail, in a later session. Hell is real and is not a manifestation of the mind.

Q. Dan. In the spirit world, do they have good and bad days as we do on earth?
A. Thomas. Yes. When you have a bad day, he Thomas, has a bad day. He is striving for perfection. When he feels he lets you down he gets upset. Consider a teacher student relationship, "If the student fails to learn, the teacher fails to teach." Don't think he is perfect, but he Thomas is The Great Communicator.

Q. Dan. Do they experience physical pain in spirit?
A. Thomas. You can choose to experience pleasure or pain. The soul can choose what ever experience he or she desires to experience at the moment, as the soul can choose at any moment or time to appear in a physical body or to just appear as a mist or light.

Q. Dan. Tell me about Jesus.
A. Gabreael. There are many questions about this. I am seeing sand and I don't know, I can't explain what I am seeing. I guess what I am seeing is what happened at your hypnosis session today. Thomas is saying that there are many questions about this.

Q. Dan. During the hypnosis session today just before this session, I met with Jesus at the Sea of Galillee. Is that what Thomas is referring to?

A. Thomas. Yes. There will be more information about this in future sessions.

Q. Dan. Was the information I received under hypnosis today, factual?

A. Thomas. Yes.

Gabreael. That is funny. You know what I was telling you about my ex-husband, Thomas is bringing that up. Thomas is saying that you can spot a karmic relationship by the hold it has upon you. "What it was, it will be again." Well that's just dandy. I am getting the finger from Thomas like, no, no, you have been so bad. Like naughty.

Sometime before this session, Gabreael had explained to me that she had a terrible experience with her first husband. When they first met and before they married, it seemed like a match made in Heaven, that they were soul mates. Once they married, the relationship became strained. There was an apparent struggle for dominance and the end result was a very bitter divorce.

Q. Dan. Was the ex-husband of Gabreael's a manifestation of the soul as he has explained to us? A manifestation of the self?

A. Gabreael. Well he is quite the poet today. "What it was, will be again." He is saying stop it, you are being bad.

Q. Dan. The soul mate that Gabreael has just mentioned, her ex-husband, was that the other half of her soul that has incarnated as a male?

A. Thomas. Yes. This is the reason that we said before, that a lot of misinformation has been put out by many concerning this subject. This is a classic example of what can happen if the two halves meet during the same incarnation. Rarely do they become compatible and get along. A lot of damage has been done to cause confusion by those who have put out this misinformation.

It should be noted here, that Gabreael remembers very little to nothing when she is in trance. When she read the transcribed tape of this reading/session, she literally threw up. While Gabreael and her ex-husband mended this bridge years ago, this is a perfect example of a soul mate collision, where one soul or one half of the soul constantly fights the other half of the soul for dominance. To this day she and her ex-husband have a love/hate relationship.

June 17, 2002
Our 12ᵗʰ Session

Heaven and Hell

Thomas says hello.

We will discuss leadership or overseers in Heaven today, starting with the seven levels.

Levels of Heaven: Angel Overseers of the Seven Levels:

1. Gabriel
2. Zachariel
3. Anahel
4. Michael
5. Sammael
6. Zachiel
7. Cassiel

There are many providences in Heaven. There are many masses and much to govern. Everything is always in order. Dan has some questions concerning Hell. Hell has seven levels as well. Seven is the number of completion. It is not good to dwell upon Hell or the overseers or to draw them near you. Do not call them to you. Do not call yourself to their attention. Understand that Hell is like Heaven in that it is in a state of progression of the levels. The seventh level of Hell is the worst, but it is the ultimate level.

Where do you think a third of the stars reside at? As an independent government, Hell has their own governing body just as Heaven and Earth. There are seven overseers. Not a lot is known about them and you don't want to go there. The Angel Overseers of Hell are:

1. Kushiel
2. Lahatiel
3. Shoftiel
4. Makatiel
5. Hutriel
6. Pusiel
7. Rogziel

There is a lot of old writing and teaching on this subject. There is a lot of ancient and verifiable text that was given to the forefathers and the Jewish writers. There is much reading to do on this subject. Do not dwell upon Hell. DO NOT call upon them. There has been much strife because of them and not much is known about them. Do not give them power or your energy.

Satan is dual sex, as well as, God, humans and angels. There is much misunderstanding about this. The watchers got in trouble over this, which led to the great flood. This was told about in Genesis, Noah's Arc. Genesis Chapter 6: Verses 1-8.

Genesis Chapter 6: Verses 1-8. (King James Version)
The wickedness of the world, which provoked God's wrath, and caused the flood.
1. And it came to pass, when men began to multiply on the face of the Earth, and daughters were born unto them.
2. That the Sons of God saw the daughters of men that they were fair; and they took them wives of all which they chose.
3. And the LORD said, "My spirit shall not always strive with man, for that he also is flesh; yet his days shall be a hundred and twenty years."
4. There were giants on the Earth in those days; and also after that, when the sons of God came in unto the daughters of men and they bore children to them, the same became mighty men which were of old, men of renown.
5. And God saw that the wickedness of man was great in Earth, and that every imagination of the thoughts of his heart was evil continually.

6. And it repented God the LORD that, he had made man on Earth, and it grieved him at heart.
7. And the LORD said, I will destroy man whom I have created from the face of the earth; both man, and beast, and the creeping thing; and the fowls of the air; for it repenteth me that I have made them.
8. But Noah found grace in the eyes of the LORD.

Much has been given to reflect and think upon, to study upon and read upon. Go in peace. Seek in peace.

Q. Dan. Who determines who goes to Hell?
A. Thomas. We determine our own destiny. We go before a review board. We are given many chances. Be not confused with this because much miscommunication and misinformation concerning this subject. There has been a lot of soul stainage. We all have a choice to go light or dark. The Dragon (Satan) had a choice.

As a good parent you let your children make their own choices. This is a mistake. Example: Allister Crowely chose the wrong path. He led many astray. An example of what you don't want to do.

Q. Dan. Can you tell me about the Prophet Daniel?
A. Thomas. Read the Bible..Revelations.

Where much is given, much is required. More is to be given on this subject. Dwell not on darkness, because darkness begets darkness. Go in peace. Seek in peace

Universal Laws

Thomas says hello.

I am seeing like a galaxy or universe; Universal Law. He wants to discuss today, how Universal Law has affected you. We abide in Universal Law. It is when you live in the law that you grow spiritually, mentally and even physically. This is part of the soul's evolution. There has been much misunderstanding about this. Don't misunderstand what I am saying. Man does have free will but from time to time we stray from a much harder course. We can live outside of the law and from time to time man has strayed and lived outside of the law.

When you break the law, you reap what you sow. This law is perfect. God gave man law to live by. Understand that God gave man law to live by to understand life and how to live. When man strays from these laws, man becomes unbalanced. Remember sowing and reaping. The key to understanding is what Jesus said. Do to others as you would do to yourself.

You must understand and know greatly, that you are your brother's keeper in that what effects one often effects many. To think deeply upon this is very important. You Dan, when you lived in Atlantis, were lawless. They did not abide by the law in Atlantis. They chose not the path of right. Warnings, many warnings were given in that era. In a nutshell, that is why Atlantis was destroyed.

Much reaping from the sowing from that day. Do you Dan, understand what he, Thomas, has just said? You, Dan, have an inner struggle concerning faith in you from Atlantis, from that lifetime.

Q. Dan. What can I do to get rid of that?

A. Thomas. It has left a residue on your soul to this day. Even though much time has passed you still have that residue on your soul. That is why you have doubt. You have a lack of faith in the law and in God in that you have the faith of man. You will have the faith of man until you deal with this and you will have a bumpy road with communications. God will not give you your heart's desires if you do not give him yours. You are very stubborn.

You have really paid for your deeds in Atlantis. Much reaping for much sowing to take away with you. The most important gift we can do in this vessel, in our physical bodies upon Earth is to serve. The greatest gift on Earth is to serve, not yourself, but others. The greatest payment we can give is to serve others.

Q. Dan. Is there something I can do to get rid of the Atlantis connection or karma?

A. Thomas. Remember your heart's desires, your wants, if you do not give it to him, he will not give it to you. You have a real faith based issue. It is not just from Atlantis or this lifetime. In your youth, even if you did not have a rough road, you would still have a faith issue, because you are pig headed.

Q. Dan. Is there some key to reversing this?

A. Thomas. Think of it like a bad stain, a stain on the soul. It takes much scrubbing, much work to get it off. Sometimes, it takes many lifetimes. Remember, you didn't do it in one day or one lifetime and you are not going to pay for it in one day or one lifetime. He addresses free will today because you needed to understand that you have free will, and you have had many chances before and you will have more chances in the future for redemption. You only think you can depend on yourself at times. We are our brother's keepers and only when you come full circle will you understand this and not have to learn it again.

You still hold some pain and strife from this issue. It's hard to let loose and commit to this because you have a great fear inside of you. Fear does nothing but eat away. When you are ruled by the fear, you are not ruled by the law. This is why you are having a bumpy road with communications. He has heard you, but until you conquer this, it will be a bumpy road. He does his best, but he abides by the law.

Q. Dan. Is there a book or something written about the Universal Laws that I can read and study on?

A. Thomas. Yes, there are several books published on this subject. There is one that we would recommend that was written based on the Edgar Cayce readings, by Bruce McArthur. (*Your Life: Understanding the Universal Laws* is available from the A.R.E Bookstore in Virginia Beach, Va.)

Q. Dan. Can you give some of the Universal Laws?

A. Thomas. You should read the book on Universal Laws to more fully understand them because they are somewhat involved. We will give you just a few of them so you can better understand.

The Law of Cause and Effect

Laws of Attraction

Karmic Laws of Choice

Laws of Self

Laws of Manifestation

And there are many more. You must read about them and study them to be able to understand them completely. Then you must pray and meditate upon then to get an even fuller understanding.

Think upon this and think hard. You know inside yourself what you must do. Much has been given. Think hard. Wallow not in doubt. Go in peace. Seek in peace.

The Christ Consciousness

Thomas says hello.

Psychic abilities of various kinds at times may be irrational, unpredictable, or to the mercy of your outer consciousness. You must understand the soul evolution; the psychic evolution. It does not happen in one day, a week, or a month. It happens over periods of time. It happens as the soul evolves, as the psyche evolves. They do this hand in hand. You can't have one without the other. If there is no balance there is no order. Look at an autism; great math skill but not much more, unless you get your information from the dark side.

Not only was Allister Crowley someone in modern times that was like this, but also Jeane Dixon. Beware of a snake; a serpent. Jeane Dixon got her information from a serpent. That's why it was so laughable. She created a mess and put out a lot of false misinformation.

You must carry the Christ Consciousness in you. That is why your hypnotic session the other day went so far back, as that certainly was not your last lifetime. It was to remind you of the Christ Consciousness within you. It is painful, because you have allowed permission for your body and soul to go from a flame to a flicker. You have allowed The Christ Consciousness within you to go from a big flame to a small flicker.

Sarcasm and cynicism eats away at the soul as cancer does to the physical vessel. Have you ever seen a person; anyone who is depressive, truly healthy? You have not. The vessels body is not ravaged, their mind is. This small portion I have given to you is much to think and study upon. A key to unlocking your healing abilities and communication skills.

No guide you seek, no psychic you seek, will be able to unlock this within you. This you did alone. Thus you repair this alone. Thomas says he will be with you a while longer; a short while, as he himself is known as the communicator guide. He was assigned to you Dan, just because of this communication issue. Soon; very soon, his work will be finished. He himself, is going to take a vacation, a long rest.

Think hard on what you have received as you will receive more for a very short time as he is in a time of sowing. Your next step, the most important step for you Dan, is coming up it is coming next. Where you are concerned, it will be a time of growth. Once a seed is sown, roots must be established. The roots must be established and then from the roots the plant will start to grow. Will your crop, your work be fruitful, or will it be full of blight?

After the growth period, will come the reaping season. He says be not afraid. Reaping in this instance means receiving the benefit of what you have sown. He says that will be the final stage of the work.

Q. Dan. What can I do to improve my psychic ability and to know the information is valid?
A. Thomas. The key to unlocking the center of a person's body already is within you. Understand, this will not happen overnight. You didn't do this overnight to yourself and it requires patience. This happened over several incarnations, not just your last incarnation.

The lifetime with Christ that you experienced during your hypnosis session the other day, was brought to you so you can understand the connection to the Christ Consciousness again. Without seeing it with your own eyes, you would never have believed it. This was brought forth for your benefit to understand the flame. You can't blame it on this lifetime alone and you can't blame it on your parents. It happened, going back several lifetimes with you. You must understand that in order to work within the Universal Law, and to be in the Law; you must be aware of and have a burning flame that only comes from the Christ Consciousness. This applies to every vessel, ever person, every soul.

A house is a vessel and a house is not built in a day, nor was the soul evolved in a day. Always remember, that everything starts as a thought form. If you don't remember anything else, remember how important what he is about to say is. Understand that everything that comes to pass, was first a thought. Your soul was first a thought. Everyone's soul was at first a thought. Before a word is spoken, it is a thought. Remember this in all things. Even if it's not spoken, it is recorded. All thoughts are recorded in the great book. All thoughts. Remember that.

Q. Dan. How long will Thomas be with me?
A. Thomas. For a while, if needed. No date has been put on it. Understand, he will communicate with you for a while. The work must be done from the seeds that have been planted. Then you will reap the harvest.

Q. Dan. You mentioned Jeane Dixon and something about a snake. Could you explain that a little more?
A. Thomas. Jeane Dixon got her gift or her information from a snake. Believe me, this happened to her. Guard yourselves. Where there is light, there is darkness as well. Look at Job. Job was allowed to be tested. Great people are always tested as your spirit guide can't tell you about all things. Some things you must learn for yourself. You must choose some things yourself. Remember this warning.

You, Dan, when you were younger, had this cross your path just a little. But what you are experiencing right now is really big and it is a great gift. All gifts are tested. He, Thomas, doesn't have much longer with you, but he wants to tell you not to be afraid.

Q. Dan. Is Thomas talking about the lizard people, the Paladins?
A. Thomas. Consider the source. You have free will. He cannot tell you all things. Some things you must choose for yourself. He says you have been warned. You Dan, know the right course to take.

What Thomas was referring to was, when I was just starting to get involved with metaphysics, I did discover the different energy fields available. Both dark and light, and I did experiment with the dark energy for a while. I learned quickly that while you could use the dark forces to control people and events, you also accumulated karmic baggage or karmic debt. I quickly separated myself from the dark side and worked only with the light.

Later on in life, I did become aware of the Pleiadians and their energy field. I did study their energy for a while, but I never really became connected to them. While I wasn't sure, I always had a feeling that they were from the dark side. As Thomas said; we do have a choice of free will to work with the light or the dark forces and it should be obvious that many choose the darkness.

Q. Dan. The mess that has been created in the Catholic Church, how does that fit in with the Universal Laws?

A. Thomas. The Priests have allowed their flames to go out. When the flame goes out, darkness enters. Remember that God would have no part in such a thing. Remember that man has free will, but they will pay for what they did. Much damage has been done. This has nothing to do with sex. This was an act of violence, a control mechanism, trying to control others when you cannot control yourself.

Go in peace. Seek in peace. Speak in peace.

Prayer and Meditation

Thomas says hello.

As he starts today, he wants you Dan, to understand that the information that is given, is chosen. He goes through a process to decide what should be given and in what order and then he communicates it.

Today, he is having a rough time communicating because of the weather. Some of what will be given, are things you have asked about. Not all questions will be answered. Some are not meant to be answered at this time, as some are for you to discover for yourself. Some of the information Thomas has given are things that need to be revealed. He expects all of it to be treated with the same degree of respect. He wants to place great importance on this because this is important to him. He himself, does not play around or play games. The information and communications he has to give can be life changing to many. The information is truly a great gift. He says it is to be treated as a great gift.

Today, he will discuss meditation. Not much more discussion will be on meditation; however, it is one of several keys, not only to psychic awareness, but to human creativity as well. You must understand, that meditation is a sister to prayer. A person should accompany one with the other. Understand, they should go hand and hand. This is very important for everyone to understand. This is a big factor. Prayer should accompany meditation. Many people misunderstand this.

I know you have some questions about this. How can you pray to someone you do not know or you do not understand? Can you pray to someone you do not know? How can you pray to someone you hold resentment for? You can't. No you can't. For most people, meditation is only 10 to 50% productive, because they do not recognize the Christ Consciousness or what it even means. Many in America are resentful. That is why America is in turmoil today. Abuse, addiction, and murder are because of the lack of the Christ Consciousness. A lot of parents do not sow or plant these seeds and mainly because they themselves do not fully understand the Christ Consciousness or even the importance of it.

Now, those without Christ, those that have children that have grown up and have begot or begat others. What man has done; he and he alone has done to himself. You cannot and you must not blame God. It is very important for proper seeds to be sown or your harvest is not going to be plentiful. When souls are reincarnated, you, that soul is given God's best. It is a great reward of sorts. You are given the best of the best; even the prodigals are given the best of the best. Prodigals that stray away are given the best and allowed to stay.

He Thomas, understands that some, but not all of what has been and is to be communicated; you may not like or agree with, but at the same time it is what is needed. It is what is revealed and it is the truth. As in all things, where there is truth there is freedom. In truth there is knowledge. Some of the information that has been given so far and some that will be given in the future, may test your religious and moral understandings or may be contrary to what you might have read or heard, but all of what has and will be given is the truth and it is what is needed to be heard and understood at this time.

Go in peace. Speak in peace. Seek in peace.

While this was a very short session, it is an important one because it reveals that some of the keys to life are prayer and meditation and above all, the ability of the soul to recognize the Christ Consciousness. Once the individual soul has made the connection to the Christ Consciousness; this opens the door and prayer and meditation are what keeps the door open. These are the very basic steps in life whether the souls is incarnate or discarnate. There is no distinction between the two. Prayer and meditation go together. One will not work without the other.

July 10, 2002
Our 16ᵗʰ Session

Spirit Guides and Environmental Influences

Thomas

He is well rested today. He has taken a well deserved rest.

Today he wants to touch upon spirit guides. He has barely skimmed or even touched the surface on this issue. Guides should be thought of as grandparents that are trying to help steer or guide us down the correct road or path. Not as a hierarchy that is untouchable; which is a common thought today.

There is thought that spirit guides have never incarnated or had only lived a few lives, as they are so much more highly developed than humans. Hogwash he says. How on earth can any person guide you through something; a bad experience or good experience or any experience; with no experience of their own at all? Hogwash, they cannot.

Human souls were created equally. It is only through soul evolution that one can become a guide. If anyone tells you; my guide has never lived before or my guide has only lived once or twice hundreds of thousands of years ago, consider the source. I Thomas, say that a person needs to consider their source. How on earth could that be possible? It cannot, even from a simpleton's mind. It makes no sense.

Often this is a person's imagination and other times it is a darker source. Spirit guides, contrary to most popular beliefs, are not perfect. Nor are they all knowing. Believe it or not, we spirit guides, do make mistakes. As far as he Thomas knows, God is the only one that is perfect and all knowing 24/7. Remember that. If we spirit guides were perfect, why is the world in such a mess? Always remember; we spirit guides were once human too we are not untouchable or unattainable.

Guides may communicate in various ways at various times. You Dan, are lucky. You are fortunate in that I Thomas, am a great communicator. Some communicate in the dream state, others communicate like me, Thomas. I may be channeled; which is not as common. Some communicate through meditation. Some spirit guides find it hard due to human experience to communicate through meditation. Others do it through environmental influences, which is most common. Little is said about environmental influences. Some examples of environmental influences are as such. You run into the same stranger several times that you do not know; a book or the same book falls at you three or four times; the same name of a place or person you may hear over and over. These are environmental influences. These are the most common of communications from the spirit guides.

Later; the next time or next discussion, we will discuss more upon this subject.

Q. Dan. Is the book on Universal Law that I got from the Edgar Cayce/ A.R.E., the information that Thomas wanted me to read?
A. Thomas. Yes, that information was for your own personal experience to pull from within yourself. A reminder for you, Dan, because you already knew about this information in other incarnations. Did you not find it as a reminder?

Q. Dan. Once I start putting the book together, will I be given additional information to fill in the blanks?
A. Thomas. What was needed, was given. What will be needed, will be given.

Q. Dan. Where are we going with all of this information?
A. Thomas. Transcribe it. Write it together. We, Dan and Gabreael, are an example of the environmental influence. We work well together as a team. When he Thomas, leaves for a while, we will still be a team because, he, Thomas, is The Great Communicator.

Q. Dan. What time frame are we looking at to receive all of this information?

A. Thomas. When all that is needed is given, there will be a time for rest. Patience little one. Not too much longer; not years, but for a while.

July 11, 2002
Our 17th Session

Dreams and Souls

Thomas says hello. This morning Gabreael's energy is scattered all over. He is telling her to focus. Not to worry about tomorrow (Gabreael is having her wisdom teeth pulled tomorrow). He will pop in to see her tomorrow while she is at the dentist.

Yesterday, he discussed environmental influences. He was fussed at by the others, so today he will discuss dreams. He feels environmental influences are the most common communication from the spirit world. However, other guides feel dreams are more important. So they have decided that one is as important as the other. He said to remember that guides are not perfect.

Dreams are the state where the subconscious takes over the vessel and the soul awakens. The soul gains total consciousness. Dreams are the experience the soul has often as we sleep. Deeply imbedded in your soul are many secrets. The human vessel holds the soul and the key to many things. Such as, past lives, lessons learned, karmic debts and your charted course and such. It holds your soul review, your life experience of the day as you first go into sleep. Then the dreams are used for instructional and educational uses during your altered state. In the dream state, the soul is without any doubt that we create our reality. That is why dreams often feel real to us when we are asleep, until we awaken. Because there is a reality to fill. Gabreael understands this well in the conscious state and applies it to her regular daily life, as She often listens to her soul and her guides.

Often as well, during a psychic experience, the average person may get glimpses into the future in their dreams. The soul and the subconscious mind lead to the conscious reality. Do not confuse these psychic influences with daily review, as they are different and separate, as well as, suggestive dreams from your soul and your guides. So remember not to confuse this. Remember that dreams are real experiences. Real experiences of the soul. The western culture doesn't acknowledge this. The evaluation your soul makes while you are asleep is what is used by your guides and your soul to help guide your future. This covers a lot. It covers a lot of questions and explains much.

Q. Dan. Thomas has mentioned for two days in a row that "Spirit guides are not perfect." Is he trying to tell us something that perhaps we have received misinformation along the way?

A. Thomas. The information that has been given recently about the Spirit Guides is valid, however a lot of misinformation has been written or given by many, especially in the last 20 years. Many current authors are channeling and not speaking through their guides. Spirit guides do make mistakes in several ways. Not often, but it happens. It is after reflection of the soul they guide, that this becomes a realization. An example of this. Someone may be meant to be a doctor, a medical doctor, however in the conscious state they get tired, scared or lazy. They can get all of these. So they become something else. A nurse, an x-ray or lab technician, whatever. But perhaps the guide could have been more persistent. Sometimes guides cannot prevent things from happening. Somethings such as karmic indebtedness and chosen paths, guides cannot change or cannot intervene. This is why sometimes bad things happen to good people and small children, the little ones. Thomas says, this is because sometimes things are for karmic indebitness and sometimes a chosen path. Everything is not karmic. Somethings have to do with evolution.

Q. Dan. Sometimes we are faced with situations or experiences that we might see as negative or bad. Are these situations things that we choose to experience before we incarnate?

A. Listen and pay attention. He has covered that. Pay attention. What is needed will be given. A great gift has been given. Remember that a life is but one season. Go in peace.

Dreams, Incarnations and Charting

Thomas

Thomas says hello. He is aware that you Dan, have several questions and he will answer them later. Now that you understand how dreams are used to tune up your chart, he wants to discuss your actual charting since this is what makes one who they are. On the other side; in spirit; you will first go through a review or prepatory process to make sure that another incarnation at that time is what the soul truly needs. Sometimes at that point; souls, after much reflection turn back and take up another task or job before reincarnating again.

Then after the preparatory review process, you will go through a long orientation process. At this point you will first start by choosing or picking your life paths. You choose two lifetime paths at that time. A primary and a secondary path. Your primary path assigns the basic goal of your upcoming incarnation. Your secondary deals with conflict you set up to overcome in this lifetime. The more conflict you overcome the more you learn.

Then you have a major and a minor obstacle or obstacles that you build into your chart. An example of this is, you Dan; your major obstacle was family. In the mean time, your minor obstacle is health. You Dan, chose this chart just as Gabreael chose hers. Your major life path is spirituality or religion while your minor life path is love and healing. Love is one of the hardest obstacles to work out.

Next there are Exits.

Exits are circumstances or situations we place in our chart to end that incarnation. The average chart has seven exits. He Thomas, has seen this differ from chart to chart, but not as often. Seven exits or outs simply mean, seven different or possible ways to exit out or return to spirit . Needless to say, your soul doesn't exit out all seven ways.

An example of this is what happened to Gabreael a couple of weeks ago. She hit, or by accident; happened upon an exit while she was in the dentist's chair, but was reminded that her soul had not accomplished or finished her chart goals. So back down she went.

Next time we will finish up the charting process. Now he will answer your questions.

Q. Dan. Since my primary obstacle was family and secondary health, have I completed those two issues?

A. Thomas. You Dan, had a rough road or path to follow, but you chose it during your charting process. You have overcome a great obstacle so far. However, there are still some underlying issues, but you are doing very well in that area. Health issues have been your focus of late. This stems from previous incarnations. Remember that this is a lifetime progress. Health is what you Dan, are working on now. Only you can do this. Remember you choose it. We need to remember that we literally bring things, circumstances and obstacles, upon ourselves.

Q. Dan. Is it possible to live two separate life paths at the same time in the same incarnation?

A. Thomas. You must understand that you always; in each incarnation; live a primary and a secondary path. That is why you can reflect back through your lifetime.

You are two different people, yet the same. You Dan, have remained in the same vessel yet looking or reflecting back; an entirely different attitude or person. There was a change at age 30 and again now. He Thomas, has given you enough information to last several years. You must understand that this is a great gift.

Q. Dan. I understand what you just said, but I have been told that at the birth of the soul, the soul splits in two and one half is female and the other half male and in a lot of cases both halves take on a separate physical body and live two separate and unrelated lives. Is that true?

A. Thomas. Yes that is possible. That is where the term "soul mate" comes from. More will be given on that subject at a later session. Everything must be in order and given in the right time frame.

Q. Dan. Does one pick or choose ones parents while charting?

A. Thomas. Yes, the individual does choose his or her parents during the charting process as well as many other things to experience.

Q. Dan. What other things are you talking about? What are some examples?

A. Thomas. Life styles, general body structure or appearance, issues one might choose to work on, things like this.

Q. Dan. Are you saying that one chooses to he heterosexual or homosexual before coming into an incarnation?

A. Thomas. Yes, those are life choices the soul can choose to experience.

Q. Dan. What about being fat or thin?

A. Thomas. As I said before, one chooses body structure or appearance, a vessel to begin each incarnation with. One chooses this during the charting process. What one does with his or her vessel during each incarnation is up to the individual.

Q. Dan. Before my birth, my mother had a baby that was still born. Is that soul and my soul one and the same?

A. Thomas. Yes, but you already knew that.

Q. Dan. Sometime ago, another psychic told me that someone close to me was going to die and that I should not try and hold on to them and keep them here. Can you reflect on that?

A. Thomas. Some people tune into a lot of babbling. There is no order in babbling. You must consider the source. If someone gave you a death date, they are breaking the law. Guides like him are never to reveal an exit. It leads to confusion, babbling, mixed emotions and such. While other guides have done this, they have been reprimanded. You must consider the source.

Q. Dan. I recently commissioned an artist in Australia to do a painting of one of my guides. Is the picture I have a picture of you Thomas?

A. Thomas. No, it is of another. He Thomas, found it interesting. This is the one they call Eon. This is a spirit guide who is on the low end of the totem and one of your spirit guides. You have several more spirit guides as well. Eon deals with dreams, turmoil, reflection and such. He Thomas, will be assigned to work with you until the information for the book is given, then Eon will be working with you for a while as well as other guides.

Go in peace.

Charting; Murder and Suicide

Thomas

He says hello.

Before he starts on charting, he wants to address a question you have. He wants you Dan, to understand that he Thomas, is The Great Communicator. He Thomas, will be assigned to you for a short while longer, then another guide will take the reins. He Thomas, was assigned to you to channel through Gabreael, through his connection with her. She, Gabreael is a procrastinater and needs a helper to keep her going. You Dan, are that mover, that person, at this time.

Always remember; where much is given, much is required. Gabreael often forgets this. Now, today, he will continue discussing charting. He may or not finish because there is much work, much information to be given on this subject.

Previously he discussed:

1. The Preparatory review process, which is simply a process to make you sure that you are ready to incarnate.

2. The Orientation process equals choosing two life paths. First a primary and then a secondary path. Hopefully, you will complete both of

them. Primary equals basic life goals, the secondary is for the conflicts to overcome. There must be no confusion about this work.

3. This stage is major and minor obstacles to overcome. He, Thomas, believes you understand this one.

4. Where he left off was Circumstances or Exits we place in that chart to end that lifetime. You usually place at least seven separate exits in your chart to end that lifetime. Before he discusses exiting any deeper, you must understand there is much misunderstanding about suicide. There seems to be a current thought in today's world that suicides get sent back immediately to earth or get sent straight to hell. This is hogwash. Neither of these are true. Anyone, any guide, any soul who tells you this is simply babbling. Please understand that everyone; every soul, please understand; he means everyone, will have at least one suicide exit in their chart for that incarnation. Some may have several suicide exits in their chart.

Why, you ask. If that was not the case, how could one soul ever guide or console another soul who is going through that very circumstance without ever experiencing that for him or herself? He, Thomas, knows this will rattle some cages and upset a lot of people but this is the truth and it is time that the truth comes forth about suicide even if it does upset a lot of people. All one has to do, is think about your own life on earth.

We all have had at least one if not several times during each life, when we hit discouraging circumstances, where one has considered opting out or considered suicide. How could you possibly console anyone else if you have never experienced that for yourself? You could not. It is as ridiculous as a spirit guide being someone that has never lived before on earth or only once or twice.

So the thought that the soul is sent immediately back into an incarnation or sent to hell, is plain hogwash. How could any soul be sent right back; as hard as it is; as much work as it is; just to go through the charting process and get into an incarnation correctly? He swears that some people will believe anything. They read or have been taught to believe this as being the truth and it is not. In truth there is always freedom.

When loved one's that have been left behind hear this, it will help to comfort those souls. Very often they blame themselves for that loved ones death. They should not. Often, society blames them. Society, co-workers and friends, often blame some of the loved ones. I say, blame no one. Suicide is just part of the charting process and no one must take any blame for this. Another myth is that there is a penalty to pay to God for committing suicide. Again, this is misinformation and is not true. There is no penalty to pay to anyone for committing suicide because the individual is the one that chose to put it in his or her chart in the first place.

Now we must discuss the exit called murder. This one will definitely rattle some cages; even more so than the suicide option. Sometimes, but not always, this is pre-ordained or chosen in the chart. He Thomas, knows many will find this disturbing, but it is the truth. Usually, but not always, it is a karmic debt, but sometimes it may be an experience the soul has chosen. It can also be considered another form of suicide in some cases. It can also be a violent act and that is where it becomes a karmic debt.

Jesus said, many times, the one thing that God the Father hates most, is the shedding of innocent blood. He says that is so for two reasons:

1. It creates a karmic debt to another soul and we should strive not to be in debt to any man, to any soul.

2. All blood that is shed is not as innocent as it may appear. In some cases it is due to a karmic payback. He Thomas, knows that this will disturb many. This will upset a lot of people and challenge their religious and moral beliefs. But think of it this way. When Cane slew Able in Genesis; this was clearly the shedding of innocent blood in the most basic of forms; thus making a perfect example of a karmic debt; a payback between these two souls, as Able had done nothing to Cane.

Further on in your old testament; Genesis: Chapter 7 to be exact; you have God the Father, murdering the whole planet with the exception of a few folks or souls. Was this innocent blood being shed? No it was not. It was an example for us, of serious karmic indebtedness being paid back.

At that time, not many souls were on the planet. Those souls at that time were very, very young. They were prideful, boastful, given in to animal and carnal primate lust time after time. The only way to purge this, was for God the Father to cleanse the earth with a flood. The water was also a symbolic form as well as cleansing. Those souls were not innocent, and certainly straightened up after that.

Another biblical example of this, between just a couple of souls, can be found in 2nd Samuel, Chapter 11, where David coveted Bathsheba, thus sending her husband Uriah to the front lines in battle. There he was murdered, creating a karmic debt between he and David. Not the man who actually killed Uriah, as he was simply doing his job in battle. It was David who plotted and schemed to get Bathsheba and place her husband in harm's way. The shedding of his innocent blood; his murder; was only on David's hands.

Everyone, all people; must remember that David was a man after God's own heart. Thus showing us that all of us have struggles, conflicts, obstacles, and such to overcome. Only the one called Christ was born perfect; in perfection in the Father. These are some excellent examples for all to ponder upon.

Q. Dan. Because of the importance of what you just told us, I want to make sure I have a complete understanding of some of the things you said. Are the life paths and obstacles two different and unrelated things?
A. Thomas.
1. Prep review.
2. Orientation; life path; both primary and secondary.
3. Major and minor obstacles to overcome.
4. Exiting.

Q. Dan. It appears that a lot of misinformation has been given about suicide and again I want to make sure that I fully understand this issue. When the soul prepares his or her chart before each incarnation; at least seven exits are built into each chart and suicide is just one of these exits and there is no penalty to pay; no sending the soul straight to hell and no sending the soul immediately back into another incarnation for punishment. Is this correct?
A. Thomas. Yes, that is correct. There has been much misinformation given by many about this issue. There is a well known psychic medium that is currently communicating a lot of misinformation about suicide.

This psychic medium has quite a following and has done a lot of damage by telling people that souls that commit suicide are sent straight back into another incarnation. Hogwash. This is not so. This psychic medium has done a lot of damage by telling people this. It has caused a lot of confusion and heartache for many.

Suicide is just another exit or means of ending an incarnation and returning to spirit, which is where we all start at when the soul is created. It is nothing more than that.

Q. Dan. When the soul chooses his or her chart, are there any mistake pregnancies or are abortions used as an exit?

A. Thomas. I will answer your question with a question. How could anyone console someone who is going through that experience if they have not been through that experience themselves? They cannot. Normally, abortion is not a common occurrence, but there have been some instances where this has been planned or charted. There are some mistakes like rape or incest that are not pre-planned. It is important that you understand this.

Thomas is saying that the vessel is getting weak now. He must go. He will finish charting in the next session.

July 30, 2002
Our 20th Session

End of Charting

Thomas.

Today he will finish charting. First a quick review.

1. Prepatory review process.
2. Orientation process.
3. Major and minor obstacles.
4. Exiting.

He wants us to understand why he Thomas, chose to discuss the murder and suicide exits. This is simply because they, murder and suicide, are the most misunderstood in all of our society. Many of the exits chosen by a soul, will be by sickness or illness. We, the soul, pre-plan them and earth pre-ordains them, because earth has become a diseased planet, thus making disease and sickness the most popular or most common exits.

Once again, an example. How could anyone console another about colon cancer if one has never experienced that disease or at least at some point had some form of cancer? You truly could not understand what that soul was going through.

The second most common sequence of exits on earth are what you call accidental death. Examples of these are car wrecks, falls, drowning and so on. Many times when a vessel is going through an accident they hear a voice internally or externally or a calming presence or perhaps a presence with them saying, do this, do that, calming them and such. Then afterward they say, if I hadn't had that experience, that calming voice, they would not have survived the accident.

That voice; that presence; is your spirit guide at that time, advising you. If they, the guides, had not had that emotional experience them-selves, how could they possibly have helped that vessel keep a cool head and their senses in that experience? They could not.

He Thomas, feels that he has covered charting pretty well for now.

Now he must, doesn't want to, but he must address some personal issues. He Thomas, wants us to understand that the information he and others have given, and will be giving to us, is a great gift to be taken seriously. Not to be played with or misused.

This information is to be taken very seriously and not for granted, as it is a great gift. It is important for you Dan, and Gabreael, to know that many were considered for this job, but the two of you were chosen. This work was pre-ordained. He Thomas, is accountable for the information he gives us, just as we two are responsible or accountable for how we use it.

Until this information is placed into written word or form; a book; It is to be guarded as you would guard a rare, most precious artifact. The work is in an infancy stage at the present time. Soon it will be out of the infancy stage. Until it becomes a matured state; it shall remain; is to remain; in a guarded state. I must put a real emphases on this. This information is not to be shared with anyone; no one until it becomes full circle. He Thomas, will let us know or make us aware when that has happened; as we should understand this without he Thomas, address-ing this as he would address a child.

Once it has come full circle, it will be published to the masses. Under-stand, this is a great work of art. You Dan, and Gabreael, must treat it as such. No great work of art is to ever be disclosed or unveiled until it is finished. You, Dan, need to understand this and consider this carefully. Remember always, the old adage: "Loose lips, sink ships." This applies to you. This applies to this work, so remember to guard this work as if it is a precocious artifact. You will only be asked to hold your silence for a while. Gabreael does not understand what or why he is addressing this issue. You Dan, do understand this.

He Thomas, goes into great depth planning this work. He will never jeopardize this work in any manor. One can jeopardize himself with loose lips. So remember, tell no one or anyone else until it is published in black and white. This means not discussing it, chatting about it, and such. This work was given for many or all peoples consumption. But it cannot be discussed or released until the time is right, which is coming soon. You have but a short while to hold on. Remember; if he Thomas, does not see what goes on, he is informed by others of any and all things concerning this work.

He will spell it out plainly one more time. This work is to be published by you two. It is for publication, not for public speaking. That is why you two were chosen. If you review the work, you will see less and less of your personal information and more work or information for the book given from here on.

We are starting to come out of the infancy stage. Now there must only be the work, which is a great gift. He Thomas, is not your father. He is not your babysitter. He, Thomas, is The Great Communicator and your guide at present. He does not like to be placed in the position of scolding. Do not place him in that position again.

Go in Peace and speak not.

Much has been given; much to reflect on today. He is not taking questions today.

August 9, 2002
Our 21ˢᵗ Session

Heaven and Hell

There is a bad storm in North Carolina today and communications are somewhat difficult with the spirit world.

Thomas says hello. He Thomas, understands that you Dan, are anxious for information but remember, anything worth having is not only worth working for but is worth waiting for as well. Communications are difficult for Thomas today because of the storm.

In the session on June 17ᵗʰ, he left off with the seven overseers of hell. He will cover the Angels of Punishment and the fallen ones, known as the Watchers. He Thomas, wants to make clear that angel worship in any form is wrong. You; all people; need to plainly and clearly understand this. They, the angels are mostly messengers; enforcers; rewarders; overseers: and Guardians for God. This must be made plain for everyone to understand. In the Bible, Colossians: 2-17 makes this plain.

Angels go against the logic of modern man and of modern science. That is why there is such a fascination with them. He Thomas, has told you much about the other levels and the other side, also known as heaven to people on the earth plane, and some about hell. What he has not told you is exactly where hell is. This could be a subject all unto itself. He Thomas, does not care to discuss this subject at this time in great depth; but he would not have us ignorant on the subject. The truth about this will shock and upset many people. Others will know it to be an ancient truth.

Hell can be found in a physical location. It is not a state of mind. Hell is located in the Northern Region of the different levels of the other side of Heaven or what ever you want to call it. Think as Heaven as the right hand and Hell as the left. They are side by side. This is ancient knowledge that can be found in the Testament of Levy; Enoch II; reference Barouch, and Apocalypse 3 like a Bruch #3.

Understand, that angels, whether corrupt or in the Grace of God, are always under God's control. Do you Dan, understand what he is saying? Even when they are performing directly under Satan.

Thomas says you Dan, have a question.

Q. Dan. God created hell as a balance, is that correct?

A. Thomas. Evil is an instrument of God. He uses it for his own Divine purposes.

Angels like human beings were created with free will. That is why there are fallen angels as they had free will and abused it.

Q. Dan. I understand the statement that "God allows Hell as an instrument for his own Divine purpose," but my question is; how does that affect the individual if God allows evil to take place? Is God just trying to see what the individual will do with free will?

A. Thomas. Job; the Book of Job; is an excellent answer to this question. Understand that man has free will as well. He says that angels are immortal but not eternal. He says this will go against many peoples grain. He is saying to read Genesis 6-6 regarding this. He said that Moses, concerning Hebrew text, Moses slew or killed and angel named Hemah. This is a well known Hebrew legend. A legend is history that has been long forgotten. Read Genesis 6-6.

Q. Dan. How does one get sent to or end up in hell?

A. Thomas. That is decided by a Counsel of Elders when the individual passes back into spirit and goes through a review process.

There is much to think about much to study about...

Go in peace.

Angels and Religion

Eon

Eon: Thomas is not here today. He is at a going away party for someone that is going off into an incarnation.

Hello. I am Eon. He is present here. He is filling in for Thomas today. Time is a concern for you Dan. He Eon, does not understand this. Truly there is no time. What was is and what is, was, and will be again. Life is a never ending cycle. They, over there in the world of spirit, do not mention time clocks or run by a schedule.

He wants to address something. He wants to address the picture you have of him. You Dan, must understand, the woman painted an interpretation of him. He Eon does not find it flattering at all. The picture has a horrible skin tone. He looks like a mutant. Discard it. If you ever see someone, anyone who looks like that over there on Earth, run for your life.

In the spirit dimension, they are in form just as they were in life. Sometimes in completion, or a true form of many lifetimes. However, often times, they take form of their last vessel, especially when appearing to those on the earth plane so as not confuse those we left behind.

He will be in and out with Thomas for a while. You Dan, have a busy week ahead of you; a hectic mess to deal with.

There still seems to be some confusion about angels. Angels do not communicate verbally, psychically, or symbolically with humans on a daily basis. There is much confusion and misinformation on this issue. Angels are messengers. Angels are protectors, and angels are enforcers. He Eon is very respectful of angels. They work hard. They are also known as the silent ones. Angels are not to be worshipped. There is much angel worship in the American society. It is ridiculous and confusing, and some of it comes from the dark side. The dark ones have done this to cause confusion.

Angels assignments are handed down the hierarchy from the hand of God. Many humans never ever see or hear an angel. The ones that do, view it is a special experience. It is rare. Not common at all. Everything in the universe is in order. Angels carry out those orders, keeping order from the hand of God. You Dan, and others; all people must understand this. There are dark ones who would love to interfere with the work you are accomplishing. Do you understand what he is saying to you?

Sometimes it is difficult to determine if the information you are receiving is coming from a light or dark being or source. Sometimes it is neither. Sometimes it is a hopeful or wishful imagination. However, test the spirit. When an angel communicates, they always appear to you in form; always. This is well documented. Not only biblically but historically in many texts, in many nations. Put it on a practical basis. When in history; anywhere, any continent, anytime, have you seen documented proof or historical proof, of an angel communicating and not appearing? You will not find one. That is why it is always written when an angel appears in a dream state or a vision to the person. It is very rare for an angel to appear in person.

The dark ones like to play games. Since they were once angels, they know how to manipulate the human experience. They have got America almost to a point of angel worship, as the dark ones desire worship. You must understand that a dark angel is not ugly. They look much like any other angel in appearance. There is much misunderstanding in the media about this. He, Eon, understands this is a lot for you, Dan, personally, to think about. Thomas will address it further with you as he is The Great Communicator.

Q. Dan. How do you know if the info you get is factual or from a dark one or if you are just making it up?

A. Eon. Angels do not channel. Guides channel. Angels are silent. This information has been handed down in all cultures in all societies. Man was created just a little bit below the angels, however some humans still try and worship them. This is done by the dark ones to cause confusion. Satan is not stupid. He has been plotting this for a very long time. They take however long is necessary.

He Eon, will give you an example of a dark angel. A man rolling around the floor in a seizure and an angel appearing to him. Look it up. Look at the mess it has created. This is what Islam's religion is based on. He will say no more since it is unknown to us. When we discover this it will mean much more to us. Look up the Prophet Muhammad. This is an example of how a dark angel works.

Q. Dan. Are you referring to Muhammad being a child molester and a murderer. These kinds of things?

A. Eon. Yes, but there is a lot more to it. Most of his information, or guidance came from the dark side or the dark forces. We will say no more at this time on this subject. Look up the Prophet Muhammad for yourself.

He will try and answer your other questions now.

Q. Dan. I have a question on DNA. Is DNA only in the physical body?

A. Eon. No, the DNA Genetic Code is connected to the physical body and the etheric body, the soul. Why is it; in many incarnations we have the same features? It is hard to explain. It is like a residue on our soul. This is a good question and Thomas will cover DNA in another session. There is much confusion and misinformation on this subject.

Q. Dan. We have time concerns. We need to have a time frame to schedule more sessions.

A. Eon. Thomas will pick this up later. Understand that there is an infancy stage, a maturing stage and then full maturity. In the infancy stage, you get your information. In the maturing stage you compile it. Maturity is when it comes full circle. We are approaching the end of the infancy stage. Thomas is The Great Communicator. He, Eon has a great sense of humor but Thomas is very serious with little or a strange sense of humor. Sometimes Thomas is down right temperamental as all artists are.

Q. Dan. In the July 23rd session, Thomas told me about my major and minor life paths. Can you explain this in more detail?

A. Eon. Ask Thomas about this as he Eon, does not want to step on the toes of Thomas.

Thomas will be back for the next session.

August 13, 2002
Our 23rd Session

Abortion and Life Paths for Dan

Thomas says good morning.

Did we miss him yesterday? Today he will take questions, but understand time is short. There is much work to be done, so please limit the questions. Much information has been given. What is needed at this time is what is given. At times he Thomas, has strayed from his planned presentation of the information as he is today to answer questions. He already knows most of Dan's questions, so ask them in any order you want.

Q. Dan. Give us a quick reference of time so we can schedule future sessions.
A. Thomas. I gave Gabreael a time table to schedule sessions. Gabreael will schedule around the moon cycles. Once a week, sometimes, maybe twice a week at his request until he is finished. You Dan, need to learn patience.

Q. Dan. Is abortion an exit?
A. Thomas. Abortion sometimes turns out or becomes an exit, however that soul returns back to spirit. Understand that there is a lot of misunderstanding about the fetus. Many believe that life begins when the first breath is taken. This is not so. Life begins at conception. Because at conception that chart starts. That chart is already in progress.

Abortions are not as common anywhere else as it is here in the West or in the United States. In many places; many continents; abortion is dealt with as an uncommon occurrence, but here in the United States it is common. Understand him now. When one commits abortion; not only is that woman vessel accountable for her actions, but so is the father. Everyone must understand this.

Q. Dan. Yes. While abortion is an exit, it is something the soul would not normally choose to do. Is that correct?

A. Thomas. That is correct. This happens when the human vessel wanders or strays off the path. Whenever you stray or wander, there is a consequence.

Q. Dan. Please explain DNA. Does it begin with birth of the soul or with birth of the physical body?

A. Thomas. DNA will be a reading by itself. You must understand that time; within a certain time frame this information will be given.

Q. Dan. Explain about the angels and their interaction with humans.

A. Thomas. He Thomas, had attempted to discuss angels with you, and you Dan, were not ready to hear what he had to say. You Dan, must understand something. He Thomas, is called The Great Communicator for a reason.

When information is given, it is to be given in order. The guides are not to randomly throw out information. For example; charting. He Thomas, took you by the hand, step by step by step. He attempted to do the same thing with angels, giving you their order or location. You were not ready. You cannot have just the titillating parts. He will leave you to ponder for a while. Maybe the next time he gives you information you will have the patience to pay attention to what he says. Understand, he Thomas, has the answer but you must get the answers in sequence. You must have patience. If you Dan, had patience you would have had that answer by now. Patience is required. However, you Dan, are learning patience.

Q. Dan. Are the angels guarding Hell light or dark angels?

A. Thomas. He Thomas will go back over all of that again, but he feels he has wasted time because you did not pay attention. He will start from the beginning and work through this. Thomas expects respect. Attention and patience is to be paid this time. A great gift has been given. You will be overwhelmed when he is through. If he gives you just a piece of this puzzle, you may put together the wrong picture. Some things he might or can give in random order but the important things must·be given in order.

Q. Dan. During the July 23rd session you briefly· mentioned my life paths. What is my primary and secondary life path?

A. Thomas. Your Primary life path is Religion. As you have always been seeking this but never grasping it. Your second or secondary life path has been occupations. Understand what he means by occupations. You Dan, have always felt like something did not fit. That there was always something for you to do that you had not yet done. It is because of your occupation. You were not ready for your true occupation which is writing and that will come later in your life. You asked for or chose this in your charting process, but you did not completely understand this.

You must understand these goals are things that you constantly work toward. And religion is something you have always worked for and thought about. Look at this and reflect upon it from that perspective.

Q. Dan. Eon brought up an issue about Islam. Is there a message there that we should be aware of?

A. Thomas. Eon brought up an example about how a dark angel treated humans. He, Thomas, could discuss this issue for hours but he will do it in order. He will give you that information but in order. Much damage has been done by that one incident and by that dark angel. There is much work to be done. There is much to be accomplished. Set up appointments for sessions around the moon cycle because communications are much better during that period. Go in peace; Seek in peace: Speak in peace.

August 19, 2002
Our 24ᵗʰ Session

Hell and Fallen Angels.

Thomas says hello.

Today he will discuss Hell and fallen angels, but first he wants to discuss another issue. Before, he Thomas, attempted to discuss or relay this information to you, but you Dan, thought you understood where he Thomas was going and then he went down another road. He thinks at that time you did not understand the information. You Dan, should have understood that the information was for the masses.

Some of the information that he Thomas gives you, may go against your grain and you may not like or agree with it. However, it is the truth. As with others; this information will upset many. In the future, when Thomas gives you some information, be patient, as this is what needs to be given at this time. You must understand this. This is very important to the process.

He does not have time to waste or to play around. He considers this to be serious work. This is a great gift that is being given, not only to you Dan, but to the masses as well. It is important that you understand what he has just said. He does not plan to backtrack. This is the last time he will do this, so pay attention.

He understands we are human. Today he will do a quick review of the seven overseers of Hell. Consider these Mayors of sorts.

1. Kushiel; This means Rigid One of God.
2. Lahatiel; Which he, Thomas, interprets as The Flamming One of God.
3. Shoftiel; This means Judge of God.
4. Makatiel; This means Plague of God.
5. Hutriel; This means Rod of God.
6. Pusiel; This means Fire of God.
7. Rogziel; This means Wrath of God.

Understand, while these are overseers of Hell, they are not dark or fallen angels. You: mankind, do not want to mess with these angels or overseers. Look at the interpretation of their names. That says it all. Do not mess with these angels.

Next we will discuss the Archangels of Punishment or Enforcement. They are:

1. Kezef; Angel of Wrath.
2. Af; Angel of Anger.
3. Hemah; Angel over Death.
4. Mashhit; Angel over Death of Children.
5. Meshabber; Angel over Death of Animals. Yes, death over animals. That is a whole subject to itself.

Understand one-third of the angels fell, so there are a lot of them. He cannot possibly know them all. But he is giving you Dan, some of the important ones that legends are written about. You can find more writings about these in Enoch. They are also well documented in the Book of Jubilee and in Genesis.

The angels; the Sons of God, were sent from Heaven by God to watch over man, thus entitled the watchers. It is important that you understand what watchers are. Watchers were sent from Heaven to earth to watch over mankind. They were angels, thus known to man as the watchers. Understand that angels walked beside man. Some of the watchers started living with the daughters of man, thus becoming Fallen. This is a separate falling from the one-third that I mentioned before. It is important that you understand that angels can fall from the Grace of God. There is a lot of misunderstanding and misinformation about this. The angels took wives and taught and bred. They taught arts that should not have been taught to man at that time. It was the actions of these angels, that caused the great flood.

Do not mess with or try to contact them. Their names are as follows:

1. Amaros; he taught enchantment which was very bad.
2. Araqiel; he taught signs of the earth; seasons and such.
3. Azael; he taught beautifying women; painting one's self; ornamenting one's self. Brian's poem, "Heaven to Earth," is about this one.
4. Baraqijal; he taught astrology.
5. Ezequeel; he taught knowledge of the skies.
6. Gadreel; he taught weaponry, which led to war.
7. Kakabbel; he taught science of constellations.
8. Penemue; he taught writing of the written word.
9. Sariel; he taught Moon secrets.
10. Semjaza; he taught medicine.
11. Shamshiel; he taught about the sun and secrets of the sun.

They really made a mess of things on earth. They taught man sciences they were not ready to be taught or for man to have knowledge of. A lot has been misunderstood about angels. Angels do not sit around waiting and speaking to you. There has been a lot of misinformation about them and this has caused a lot of confusion and has been part of the reason that man worships the angels. Again, man is not to worship the angels. It is very important that everyone fully understands this.

They are messengers, enforcers, and such for God. Do not evoke these dark ones. Women; earthly women, are more subject to this, as dark angels find the woman vessels attractive and being the angels are natural dominators, they can dominate the women. Much has been given, much to reflect upon. A lot of hard work is to be done by you, Dan.

Go in peace. Seek in peace. Speak in peace.

September 25, 2002
Our 25th Session

Angel Worship

Thomas says hello strangers. Before he starts off, he has some personal issues to address. He understands Gabreael's dilemma. She will feel fully up to par after Oct 6th. He wants to address something totally different. Another issue.

He has given us a great gift. It is not to be played with or taken lightly. He told us who he was and what he was. This was to be a validation of that information; giving us his historical proof. He has also informed you, Dan, that you and he did not have a previous life connection, much less a soul connection. He understands that the reading that you just received was done in jest, however, miscommunication with false representation can be extremely dangerous. It is important that you, Dan, and Gabreael understand this.

Please remember that he has given a great gift. A great affirmation of himself and his work. He knows that you have other guides, but he Thomas, knows of no George. He understands this because he has a sense of humor. That should be enough of that. Thomas is referring to a reading by another psychic, that told me I had a spirit guide named George.

Secondly and getting back to the subject. The statement he made about angels being immortal but not eternal, has made you, Dan, think quite a bit. This is one of several issues he has warned us about early on. He warned us that you may not agree with the information being given. It may go against the doctrine we were raised with. Other things he will explain more in detail in the future.

Angels are immortal; this equals not mortal; not human. You, Dan; no vessel ever dies and becomes an angel. Angels were created by God before Man. They are not eternal. Eternal equals lasting for evermore, alone. Only God is eternal alone for evermore. Without God, the angels nor us, the mortals; none on the other side, could exist. If God should perish today, they would perish instantly. However, if the angels or mortals should perish instantly, God would still exist. This puts it in the simplest, most basic context he can explain that you will understand. It is important that you; all mankind, understand this.

He gave us some Scripture before just to make us think. Genesis 24-40; Genesis 48-16; and Acts 12- Chapters 11–15. These are simple examples of angels interacting with normal human vessels. They simply do their job and leave. Understand that what he is about to reveal will go against many grains and will test the basic belief system of many, but it is the truth and must be said for all to hear.

Angels do not sit around and channel their energy. The only example of that he knows of is 2nd Corinthians Chapter 11: Verses 14 & 15. There is a lot of 2nd Corinthians going on in today's world. As it was prophesied; it would be in the latter days of man. This, we are to be weary of. This we are to stay totally away from. He, Thomas, is aware that this will bother you down deeply in areas of your soul and you and he knows why. He, Thomas, sees no need to explain further.

Know now, however, what he can say is that once the truth has been told, once you have been warned, partake of it no more. A sin is not truly considered a sin when done in ignorance. However, when done knowingly it can stain the soul. He Thomas, has given a lot of information to reflect upon today. Much to think about. He understands that some of the information bothers you deeply but it is the truth and the time has come to hear the truth. He wants you to understand that angels do not channel. Be aware of those that say they channel the angles because this is not so.

He believes he has plainly made it clear that angel worship is wrong. He will go on to something else next time. He understands Gabreael's weariness. Hang in there. October will be her month. She will know what to do then.

Go in peace. Seek in peace. Speak in peace.

October 14, 2002
Our 26th Session

Deoxyribonucleic Acid (DNA) The Genetic Code

Thomas says hello. Today he will start discussing what you questioned him about several times before. What you refer to as DNA. He knows Astral DNA. There has been a lot of rubbish printed and spoken on this matter.

First he will start by clearing up some misreprensation and untruths that are out there. There has been some misinformation channeled purposefully by the ones you know as the Pleiadians. He, Thomas, knows them as the dark ones. Anything they have to say, some parts of truth can be found in it. Because that is how the dark ones work. They take simple truth and distort it for their own benefit and amusement.

You must understand this. All men must understand this. Man has no Reptilian or Lizard in them. Anyone that would say such an untruth; you must be weary of, as they are channeling the dark side. He knows some about this and he will be glad to share with you some of what he knows to be true on this subject.

He will give you some simple basic facts; all that you need to be aware of at this time. To truly desire the company of God is to study his work. Life, is but passing through this great universe. In this process, God is transforming life.

The Kabbalah; the tree of life holds the secrets of the great ones; of God and his works.

Four Nuclei types, called; Heavanine; Satovian; Guaninine and Famine, were bound together in the same way as Sacarot. Love and power, endurance and majesty as they are bound together on the tree of life. The four are bonded together by hydrogen. All four are connected by a descending and ascending spiral called a double helix. The double helix is divided into a positive and a negative side so you actually have triple codes of sorts here.

1. Four bonded by Hydrogen.
2. Four connected ascending and descending as a double Helix.
3. The double is divided into a positive and a negative.

Now understand, that this is where it gets complicated and this is where he will stop. Simply because of this. People on the earth plane are trying to understand Astral DNA, and this is equal to trying to build a nuclear bomb in a day. It will never happen. All you need to understand here on earth about Astral DNA is that is the partner to karma. Karma is not the only reason that we reincarnate in large circles. Astral DNA plays a large part in that as well.

People in general on earth do not understand your own vessels that DNA makes up. So how could you possibly fathom Astral DNA? You simply can not. He Thomas, has given you all that he will give you on this subject. There is much else to attend your energies to.

Q. Dan. Would you please answer just one quick question to clarify something that has already been given? When the soul is created, the Astral DNA is created. When a soul enters a physical body, there is at that time, another DNA Genetic Code created for that individual body. Does some of the Astral DNA remain the same in the physical body from one incarnation to the other?
A. Thomas. Yes, that is true and this was covered in a previous session.

Q. Dan. If what was just given is true, then it would be possible through DNA to prove that the soul has in fact, reincarnated upon the earth plane more than once. It that correct?
A. Thomas. Yes, to put it in the most simple form, but you must understand that DNA is a very complex and complicated subject and even at this time, your scientists on earth do not fully understand it.

Q. Dan. Is it possible at this time or in the near future that man will have the knowledge and ability to clone other humans?

A. Thomas. Yes, this is possible now. There will be an announcement concerning this sometime in January 2003. Once man has mastered this technique; it will be the start of "The End Of Days" as revealed in Revelations. No more information will be given at this time on either of these subjects.

Go in peace.

Eon and Thomas

Thomas is present mostly for observation. He is aware of your request to go over to the spirit side, but you must understand something. You, any person in general does not choose it, it chooses you. When one is ready, one will go. Not before. You, Dan, or any vessel can request this themselves in meditation and prayer time. One does not need a medium or someone else to do it for them.

He, Eon, and your other guides; a group of guides; have been reviewing the work; the information that is being given to you. Much information has been given and more will follow. You must understand something. You have been given a lot of information as well as a lot to deal with. Take it one thing, one step at a time. It is important that you understand what he is saying.

You, Dan, personally, sometimes bite off more than you can chew. This book must be done right. This is where the focus must be. Much patience will be required. Honestly, you do not have much further to go. Much has already been done.

Last time he spoke with you, we discussed dreams and some about the angels. Today, he, Eon, feels angels have been discussed enough and he will move on. You need to understand this and focus your attention on the information that has been given to you. Shortly, you, Dan, will need to compile and organize all of the information that has been given. The information will need to be prepared to submit for publication. You will have much work to do.

Q. Dan. How can you interpret the information you receive in dreams?
A. Eon. Understand that no one remembers all dreams consciously. However, subconsciously it is as important as it is consciously. If everyone remembered all dreams consciously, there would mass confusion.

You, Dan, are always in a hurry. You must understand that you can not have everything at once. It comes with time. You personally, have ignored your dreams most of your whole life. Then, you expect all of a sudden to become all knowing. It will not happen. Next time around, pay more attention. You have been given many opportunities and you have ignored them and you knew better, as you had read about it and you have been contacted about it.

Q. Dan. Who are my other guides and what are they helping me do?
A. Eon. To avoid any further confusion, you will know what you know for now. Think of it like this. To many cooks spoil the broth. Understand that you have them, but you already have way more information than most people have. In time, all of them will be known to you. You want too much to fast. Patience is a virtue that you need to learn.

Q. Dan. Is the information credible that I received from the psychic called Jeff?
A. Eon. Know and understand that what he is about to say is very important. When dealing with this sort, with this information, always get a validation. If you do not get a validation or affirmation, let it go, release it. Always consider this in all areas. A lot of nonsense has been given to the public; to the masses. Now, you personally have grown. Now you understand. Sometimes when a person seeks, that person can desire so much that they will accept or incorporate what they want to hear into the information. He believes you understand what he is saying. He says also, understand concerning your own intuition, always look for a validation, but at the same time, they, on the other side, in the spirit world, do play parlor tricks or such. He and Thomas do not participate in such foolishness. He or Thomas or any true spirit guide will not jump through hoops as a dog.

I will give you an example of that. A well known psychic medium is telling people that suicide victims are turned around and put right back on the earth plane, this medium is channeling theirself. It is utterly ridiculous.

There were many good famous psychics. Edgar Cayce was the best. Newer ones are John Edward, who is growing and will be better as well as James Van Praagh. But more are rising, as the time has come. Always look for validation, as some psychic mediums channel darker forces. It shows in their eyes, because the eyes are the window to the soul.

Q. Dan. At what point in spirit do you become aware of the information we have just been given for this book?

A. Eon. When you return to spirit you go to an assigned level and things come to you gradually as they do on earth. As on earth, everyone, every person does not know everything at once and it is that way in spirit. You must remember that Thomas is known as The Great Communicator and the reason that the information was given to you at this very moment; at this very time; is to counteract some other misleading information that is being given out at this very time.

Did you not find it unusual; the events that unfolded in the news last week. There is much misinformation, past, present and future misinformation. That is why it is important to finish the book as soon as possible. This was to come; this is a fulfillment; this needs to be completed now.

Q. Dan. I do a lot of work with friends and relatives in the spirit dimension. Is it ok to discuss this information with them even though they may not be aware of a lot of it?

A. Eon. Yes, they are working with these issues anyway and some of the issues or situations were ones that they created and some were ones that you chose to experience and they must deal with those issues on their own time. You must also remember, that in spirit, there is no time or reference to time. You, Dan, must also understand that you cannot fix or solve everything.

Q. Dan. If the soul splits in half at the creation of the soul and both halves can and most times do live separate and unrelated lives, is it possible for the soul to split into more than two pieces and live more than two separate lives at the same time?

A. Eon. This was a question for Thomas. He, Eon, has been ordered or directed not to address the information given by Thomas. Meditate upon this while you are working on the book and you will get your answer. Thomas is testy and he, Eon, doesn't want to get on his bad side.

Q. Dan. Are Jesus and God one and the same?

A. Eon. One and two. God is the Father and Jesus is the SON. Jesus is the incarnation of God on Earth as a vessel. One and two. Jesus is an extension of God. That is the easiest way to explain the seventh level. Jesus came directly from the Father and is pure thought. Jesus was not tainted in any way. That also is the difference between Jesus and Man. The soul of man was created separately from God but is a part of God.

Thomas says he will see you next week. They both say goodbye.

November 4, 2002
Our 28th Session

End of Sessions

Thomas says hello and good morning.

He wants to start, concerning his last session on spiritual DNA. You must understand that he, Thomas, is of clear mind on this subject. Look back at your last reading in the month of March. You, Dan, specifically asked about Spiritual DNA. Thus he took the time to include it into the session.

He wants us, both of us, Dan and Gabreael, the pair of us to pay close attention to his words today and for you, Dan, to remain silent and allow him to speak. Now, right now, we approach; we are coming upon a most exciting and exuberant time. As it is now time to accumulate all the sessions into one work.

He, Thomas, understands that we are somewhat nervous about this work. Especially you, Dan. You must understand that you both were chosen to do this. Where much is given, much is required. You must understand that this is a great, great gift. This will be the hardest on you Gabreael. Fear not, what has been spoken is the truth and truth prevails in the end. He, Thomas' job was to communicate this information because he, Thomas is The Great Communicator.

It will be your job to see that this information is processed properly. Work together on this book. You will overcome all of the obstacles placed in your path. Submit the work, the book, when the time is appropriate, and it will be published. He, Thomas, will be checking in and following our progress. If he feels a need to add more on an issue, he will. But understand he does not do parlor tricks. He will not be subject to side show theatrics. We will understand this later. He, Thomas, understands that we have questions, but we always have questions.

What was needed has been given. It is important for you, Dan, to be patient, as patience is not a virtue for you. Be diligent. After this is written, you, Dan, must pay close attention to what he is about to say. After this is written it is important for you, Dan, for your family, to remain silent. He knows this is very hard for you, but you must remain silent. This is why he, Thomas, said it will be the hardest on Gabreael. You, Gabreael, must be strong. When in doubt, remember to pray and the answer will be given to you.

Remember, before you were born, before you were born into this lifetime, you chose this. Just as it choose you. You have been a martyr before as you will be again. You, Dan, are to publish the book using a pen name. You, Gabreael, will use the pen name Gabreael. I have not addressed a lot with you, Gabreael, as you are the quieter of the pair, as you are the thinker of the pair.

What I am about to tell you, be not afraid of. You, Gabreael, are about to approach a cross roads in your life. You are going to have some health issues arise. They will appear as if out of the clear blue sky very soon. They will appear during the same time you two are working on the book. Gabreael; it is most important for you to fear not as you will over come this. Assimilate the work into one work. This will mostly fall upon Dan. Questions in reference to the book are to be carried out by you, Gabreael.

I have told Dan that he will not do any public speaking, as this will be necessary for his family. This will eventually fall upon you, Gabreael, as I know in this lifetime, public speaking has been an achilles heal for you. You both will understand all I have said in time. I have enjoyed working with you two immensely. Please review all that I have said today.

Go in peace. Speak in peace. Seek in peace.

Question by Dan. Are we to assume that there will be no more topics of discussion?

You must understand that it is time to accumulate all sessions into one work. He, Thomas will check in from time to time. When he, Thomas, checks in you do not necessarily see or hear him. He has said what he was given to say. All that was needed to be said was given. Much has been given. A great gift has been given. Please understand this. It is now no longer upon he, Thomas, but upon the two of you.

Summary and Personal Opinions

July 2, 2003
Our 29th Session

Thomas & Eon

Thomas says hello and that Eon is present.

There will be no miscommunication on what he, Thomas, The Great Communicator has to say. It is not by conjecture or by coincidence that chapters 12 and 21, are the chapters that we are having issues with. It is also no coincidence that 12 and 21 are inverted on the subject matter of Hell. It was also not by chance that it was on session seven, which is the number of completion, that Thomas chose to reveal himself. Do you think that he, Thomas, The Great Communicator just handed out this information randomly?

Much work, much time, many years were put into this process. You two, you and Gabreael must understand that there are forces, darker forces out there that would rather not have this work completed, not to have this work come out.

Where there is truth, there is freedom. Session 12, where he Thomas stated was there was seven levels of Hell and that 7 is the number of completion. Hell is in a constant state of progression with the seventh level being the worst. This is where a third of the fallen ones reside.

He never meant to say that you go to Hell and get a "Get out of Hell" free card after so long. Nor did he ever say that there was a one way progression out of Hell. It is a combination of you and Gabreael's wishful thinking and miscommunication. Let there be no miscommunication , no misunderstanding upon this subject. As he told you before, this is a subject that is not to be dwelled upon, because when you dwell upon this subject you call the dark ones to you. He has seen and he has felt a dark one about. Don't let these dark ones cause you confusion. What has been has been given, what has been said has been said. Do you, Dan understand what he is saying?

Dan. I do understand, but I have a question. You said that the seventh level of Hell is the level of completion and also the worst level. My question is in two parts. The seventh level is the completion of what and once you get sent to Hell there is absolutely no way to redeem yourself and get sent back to one of the levels of Heaven. Is that correct?

Thomas. He, Thomas is frustrated because when he, Thomas chose to discuss this subject with Dan, it was meant to be session 12 . Yet Dan was not ready and Thomas had to readdress this as it is no coincidence that it fell upon session 21. Dark ones are about, conspiring to thwart this work. He, Thomas wants to make clear that after level seven, the soul in tack, does not go back to Heaven. He, Thomas has not been given permission to say anymore as he told you that not a lot is known on this for a reason.

What you Dan need to know to place in the book, is simply that there is a Hell and it has seven levels and it is a state of progression. The overseers are more of a verification or affirmation for those who read. That is what you need to place in this work. Understand that upon this subject of Hell, there are dark forces that will be drawn to this work, but he, Thomas does not want to give them the keys to the Gates of Hell. The object of this book is not to give them the keys to the Gates of Hell, but rather to plant seeds. Do you understand what he says?

Dan. I think I do. I think he said that the works of the book are not going to give enough information that would be the keys that the dark forces could use to open the Gates of Hell, is that what he said?

Thomas. Exactly, and furthermore it is to plant seeds of hope. A lot of miscommunication, a lot of trash is being printed. Many masses, a lot of people believe that there is no retribution for the way they live their life here on earth. He wants you, Gabreael, he wants all to understand that while we are given many chances at some point with each person it is different, but we do pay for our actions. Just as we choose those actions. He, Thomas, will not address this subject again.

Thomas does not want you, Dan, to dwell upon this subject any further as he, Thomas, has felt a dark one about you. He, Thomas, understands the health obstacles that you, Dan, have faced. Thomas understands that you, Dan, have learned many lessons and certainly a lesson in patience on this book. He, Thomas, is very proud of Dan's persistence. Thomas knows that you, Dan, will get the work out. He, Thomas, is saying that much will be accomplished in the time of the fall as fall comes about, as he foresees health issues and the obstacles. As he said it is no confidence that this happened in sessions 12 and 21. This is an absolute validation for Dan. Anything satanic is always inverted, that is the Dragon's way.

Dan. I have two questions. Can we use this session in the book and what can I do to dispel the dark forces around me?

Thomas. He, Thomas, does not mind if you, Dan, include this session in stating your position on Hell, but he, Thomas, by no means, wants any statement, any writing, any conjecture in the book stating that any soul may progress out of Hell by any means. No confusion, no chaotic work. Do you, Dan, understand what he said?

Dan. Yes, I have no problem with that. It is only the one issue that Gabreael and I have a disagreement about the book. If we add this session to the book with just a brief statement as to why we are adding it, I agree that I am not going to add anything else to that.

Thomas. This subject troubles Thomas much, he says. It has been reoccurring in Dan's soul history since the time of Atlantis. You struggle to overcome, but at time you stray off from your path. You, Dan, have felt what Thomas is telling you. Thomas wants you, Dan, to go into meditation using the White Light to rebuke this dark force from you in the name of the Father, The Son, and The Holy Spirit. He, Thomas, wants you, Dan, to do this for seven days. Do you understand this he says?

Dan. Yes, are you saying to rebuke the dark force?

Thomas. Yes, he says to identify it, which you have, recognize it and rebuke it, taking back charge of your home and your health. Is not a coincidence that you have had so many home issues while dealing on or with this book. Do you understand?

Dan. I am beginning to. Are you saying that all of the health issues that I have are ones that I chose to put in my chart and that some are being provoked by the dark forces?

Thomas. Many have been ones that you, Dan, have chosen, but many have been intensified by the dark ones. Do you understand?

Dan. Yes I do.

Thomas. Also it is no coincidence that Gabreael feels like a candle in the wind at this time in her life. She also needs to follow the meditation and prayer in rebuking the dark forces for seven days. Much of Gabreael's issues or problems are from stubbornness, from pig headedness and he Thomas is upset with Gabreael. Thomas is not laughing. Thomas said the Gabreael's guides have told him that Gabreael has acted badly·toward them. He says that the sad part is that she knows better. You, Gabreael chose this path, this road to walk upon, to go down. No matter how hard you try to take another path, it will simply circle back into this path. You only have fear to fear itself. Gabreael's guides are good. They are very protective of Gabreael. They have excellent communications with her. Gabreael should be ashamed for her behavior, for yelling at her guides. Do not think that Thomas does not have this displayed to him. Do not think that Thomas does not see or hear what goes on in Gabreael's mind. You can run but you cannot hide. You, Gabreael, do not want Thomas assigned to you. Thomas would teach you a good lesson. When you Gabreael do not listen to your guide named Mike, that is insulting he says. Your guides need companionship. You, Gabreael need a good spanking, a punishment he says. Do not inflict this upon yourself. Write to the ones that have contacted you. Get busy in your work. Quit veering from your path. Gabreael's husband, gives her good advice. Do not ignore it he says. Thomas does not want to have to make a personal appearance.

If he does, Gabreael will be sorry. Thomas is getting really mad now. He says that her soul, her whole soul knows what it is that she is to do, and that is why she has been tormented in the dream state and this will continue until she straightens up and walks the straight path and stops this nonsense. Gabreael wanted time to be a mother. Time was given. Mother hood is over he says.

It is time to crack the whip. There is much to be done. Much work to be about. Gabreael has been told repeatedly what it is that she is to do, and Gabreael is to do it. Work with Dan and get busy. Gabreael stays in a safety net and she needs to get out of the net.

About the Co-Author

Gabreael is an internationally renowned psychic medium. Her unique glimpse through the veil has brought comfort to the masses over the years.

For more information on Gabreael, please see:
www.gabreael.com.

Printed in the United States
19719LVS00006B/13